COLLEGE FOR HUMAN SERVICES
LIBRARY
345 HUDSON STREET
NEW YORK, N.Y. 10014

NATIONAL MIDDLE SCHOOL ASSOCIATION

Elliot Y. Merenbloom is one of the best known middle level administrators in the United States. In addition to serving as the effective principal of Pikesville Middle School in Baltimore County, Maryland, Merenbloom has conducted dozens of institutes on teaming across the country, served as a staff member and speaker for numerous conferences and has been a consultant in a host of other school districts. His NMSA monograph, *The Team Process,* has been a particularly popular publication. The first edition of the present monograph, published in 1982, has been reprinted several times to meet demand.

In light of new developments and additional faculty needs made evident through the monograph's use in the field, Mr. Merenbloom agreed to completely revise and expand it. Though retaining the original title, this second edition is really a new publication. Eight chapters have become sixteen chapters. The number of pages likewise doubled.

The Publications Committee is most appreciative of Elliot Merenbloom's commitment to the Association. His willingness to prepare this extensive manuscript is commendable.

Copyright © 1988 by the National Middle School Association
First Printing
4807 Evanswood Drive, Columbus, Ohio 43229

All rights reserved. No part of this publication may be reproduced or transmitted in any form or by any means without permission in writing from the publisher except in the case of brief quotations embodied in reviews or articles.

The materials printed herein are the expressions of the author and do not necessarily represent the policies of NMSA.

Contents

FOREWORD v
PREFACE vi

PART I: EFFECTIVE MIDDLE SCHOOLS: A CONCEPTUAL DEVELOPMENT

CHAPTER
- I.   Research On Effective Schools 1
- II.   Characteristics Of Effective Middle Schools 5
- III.   The Change Process 10
- IV.   Staff Development 16

PART II: IMPLEMENTING EFFECTIVE MIDDLE SCHOOLS
- V.   A Model For Implementing The Characteristics Of Effective Middle Schools 27
- VI.   An Effective Middle School 34
  Features A Program That Responds To The Physical, Intellectual, Social-Emotional, And Moral Needs Of Early Adolescents
- VII.   An Effective Middle School 44
  Has A Set Of Key Documents To Guide All Aspects Of The Program
- VIII.   An Effective Middle School 51
  Possesses A Definite Curriculum Plan That Includes Organized Knowledge, Skills, And Personal Development Activities
- IX.   An Effective Middle School 59
  Has A Clearly Established Program Of Studies Based Upon The Concept Of Exploration And Provides Opportunities For Student Growth
- X.   An Effective Middle School 68
  Builds On The Strengths Of Elementary Education And Prepares Students For Success In High School

XI. An Effective Middle School 73
Employs Teachers Who Focus On The Learning Needs Of
Pupils By Using Appropriate Teaching Strategies

XII. An Effective Middle School 78
Creates Teaching Teams Using Block-Of-Time To Best
Deliver The Instructional Program

XIII. An Effective Middle School 86
Emphasizes The Guidance And Counseling Function Of
Staff Members By Providing For A Home-Base Program,
Stressing The Importance Of Self-Concept, And Providing A
Positive Climate

XIV. An Effective Middle School 101
Promotes Flexibility In Implementing The Daily, Weekly,
And Monthly Schedule To Meet Varying Needs Of Students

XV. An Effective Middle School 109
Actively Involves Parents In Various Aspects Of The
School Experience

XVI. An Effective Middle School 114
Evaluates The Program On A Regular Basis And Makes
Changes That Enhance Learning

FOREWORD

In writing the Foreword to the first edition (1982) Myrle Hemingway, then a member of the Publications Committee, opened with the following paragraph:

> Leaders in group development agree that decisions produced by the group to be involved in implementing those decisions are almost always superior to decisions produced by even the most capable individual. Research carried out in industry, voluntary organizations, and schools has demonstrated that the satisfaction of subordinates increases when they believe they can influence particular aspects of the organization. People can be expected to make commitments to courses of action they helped to develop.

Since those still valid words were written a wave of school reform efforts has swept the nation. Initially, many conscientious but over-eager commissions, legislators, and boards sought to achieve school improvements by calling for more stringent standards, increased requirements, and other top-down measures. They ignored the basic principle in Hemingway's first paragraph. While such efforts received much publicity and did help to focus public concern, they have proven to be hollow. Now the realization that real reform must be bottom-up and involve teachers has emerged. In the last year or two state after state has moved to shift its school improvement thrust from a regulatory stature to one of teacher empowerment. The belief now widely held by school reform leaders is that teachers should be more involved in the decision-making in their school. School-based planning teams and instructional cabinets are being organized as alternatives to more bureaucratically based approaches to school improvement.

The appearance of this volume, *Developing Effective Middle Schools Through Faculty Participation,* is then, perhaps even more timely now than when it was first published. It is philosophically sound and most current. This monograph is not just a narrative exposition, it is a handbook that offers specific activities which can actively involve an entire faculty in implementing the middle school concept or any of the identified characteristics.

At the same time these activities will also go a long way to make up the deficit in understanding about middle level education that has plagued so many middle school faculties. Sound curricular improvement efforts become good staff development efforts. Secondary or elementary trained teachers can acquire needed understandings as they participate in meaningful school improvement programs.

This enlarged second edition is highly recommended to those schools committed to moving ahead in a critical need of our times, the improved education of early adolescents.

John H. Lounsbury
Editor, NMSA Publications

PREFACE

This second and enlarged edition of *Developing Effective Middle Schools Through Faculty Participation* is dedicated to the teachers of Pikesville Middle School and to other middle school teachers around the world who strive on a day by day basis to make these ideas a reality.

The publication is intended not only for schools making the initial transition to middle school, but also schools in the process of expanding an existing program, schools or systems attempting to establish long range goals for the education of early adolescents, schools or systems in the process of refining short term goals, and even groups of teachers within schools interested in finding out "how to get there" in a goal-setting process. The monograph is structured in such a way that it will be resourceful for all of these situations.

Developing Effective Middle Schools Through Faculty Participation is divided into two parts. Part I is an examination of the conceptual development of the effective middle school. A review of recent research on effective schools is followed by a presentation of the characteristics of an effective middle school. Part I also includes a explanation of the change process and a staff development model for successful program implementation.

Part II features a comprehensive model for implementing the eleven characteristics of an effective middle school. The model includes a process to achieve faculty participation in the implementation of each specific component. Part II may then be used as a guide to design or more fully implement each of the characteristics of an effective middle level school. The format includes a review of the conceptual basis for each characteristic, techniques to organize administrative/supervisory leadership, goal-setting procedures, and methodology for assessment/evaluation in addition to the focus on faculty participation.

This publication is dedicated to teachers because of my belief that the best way to achieve an effective middle school is to actively involve those staff members who have the responsibility of teaching pupils. If teachers are involved in developing a program, they will assume responsibility for the success of the program. Teachers develop a sense of ownership when their input is received and appreciated. This, in my opinion, is the key to the successful implementation of the middle school concept.

Two people have been extremely instrumental in producing the second and enlarged edition of this monograph. I would like to thank my wife, Ilene, for typing and retyping the manuscript, and John Lounsbury for his efforts in editing and managing the production of *Developing Effective Middle Schools Through Faculty Participation*.

Elliot Y. Merenbloom

Part I
Effective Middle Schools: A Conceptual Development

Chapter I
Research on Effective Schools

In recent years, educational leaders have felt considerable pressure to improve schools. They have looked to research for direction, and the literature on effective schools has been replete with commentaries trying to answer the question, "What is an effective school?" For the most part, the effective schools research looked at schools on a K-12 basis. Critics of this national research have accused the authors of trying to establish national norms. On the other hand, many have commented that the effective schools research simply focuses on how children learn.

In order to examine the implications of this research for the middle grades, it is necessary to review certain of the major studies. Following this, common factors will be identified and implications for middle level education will be presented.

A REVIEW OF RELEVANT RESEARCH

The late Ronald Edmonds believed that effective schools shared certain essential characteristics. According to Edmonds, the characteristics of an effective school are:
1. The principal's leadership and attention to the quality of instruction
2. A pervasive and broadly understood instructional focus
3. An orderly, safe climate conducive to teaching and learning
4. Teacher behaviors that convey the expectation that all students are expected to obtain at least minimum mastery
5. The use of measures of pupil achievement as the basis of program evaluation

In reviewing a number of school improvement projects, Edmonds identified four common factors. First, the local school was the unit of analysis and the focus of intervention. Second, teachers presumed that all school age children were educable. Third, rather than working for increased financial support, the design focused on more efficient use of existing resources. Finally, and perhaps of most importance, all of the programs used increased achievement for low income children as the measure of gain while presuming that such gains would also be true for middle class children.

Brookover and Lezotte (1979) identified a number of characteristics of effective schools. They stated that:
1. Improving schools accept and emphasize the importance of basic skills mastery as prime goals and objectives.
2. Staff of improving schools believe all students can master the basic skills objectives, and they believe the principal shares this.
3. Staff of improving schools spend more time on achieving basic skills objectives.
4. Principals at improving schools are assertive instructional leaders and disciplinarians.
5. Staff of improving schools accept the concept of accountability and are involved in developing accountability models.
6. Teachers at improving schools are not very satisfied or complacent about the status quo.
7. There is more parent-initiated contact and involvement in improving schools.

The Phi Delta Kappa study (1980) concluded that:
1. Successful schools are characterized by clearly stated curricular goals and objectives.
2. The leaders' attitudes toward urban education and expectations for school and program success determine the impact of the leader on exceptional behavior.
3. The behavior of the designated school or program leader is crucial in determining school success.
4. Successful urban schools frequently employ techniques of individualized instruction.
5. Structured learning environments are particularly successful in urban classrooms.
6. Reductions in adult/child ratios are associated with positive school performance.
7. Successful urban schools are characterized by high levels of parental contact with the school and parental involvement with school activity.
8. Successful schools frequently use staff development or inservice training programs to realize their objectives.
9. Resource and facility manipulations alone are insufficient to affect school outcomes.

In a study that examined secondary education, Rutter and others (1979) concluded that:
1. Outcomes were better in schools where teachers expected the children to achieve well.
2. Outcomes were better in schools that provided pleasant working conditions for the pupils.
3. Outcomes were better in schools where immediate, direct praise and approval were the prevalent means of classroom feedback.

4. Outcomes were better in schools where teachers presented themselves as positive role models.
5. A school's atmosphere is influenced positively by the degree to which it functions as a coherent whole.

SOME COMMON FACTORS

Throughout these studies, a number of common factors emerge. The leadership role of the principal is extremely important in establishing a climate for learning as well as a sense of order and discipline in the classrooms and corridors. The principal's major focus must be supervision of the learning process.

Beyond establishing a climate, there must be a clear emphasis on achievement as well as evidence of individualized growth in the basic skills. Teachers need to have control over instructional decisions and be keenly aware of their responsibilities for monitoring student progress. Accountability is no longer simply a school district or a local school issue; it is a responsibility of each teacher in each classroom.

It should be evident to everyone concerned that all individuals employed by the school have high expectations for student success. It has been clearly established that students are more successful when everyone in the school expects success and reinforces that belief on a daily basis.

To support such an expectation, each school must have a clear set of goals and objectives. These goals and objectives must be known to all who work and learn in that setting. The goal-setting process is a means of making improvements, not just accepting the status quo.

Parents should also be made aware of the school's priorities. They should be invited to become active participants in certain aspects of the school's program. Parents should believe in and support the school's goals and objectives. Effective communication will be a major factor in achieving this goal.

Perhaps the most common factor noted in these studies is the importance of staff development. It is clearly the role of each school system and individual school to help teachers be effective in the classroom. Many teachers have completed their graduate courses; thus, it becomes necessary to provide the additional training needed on-the-job. The effective school devotes much time and energy to the continuing development of teachers as professionals.

WHAT DOES THIS MEAN FOR MIDDLE LEVEL EDUCATION?

There are limitations to the effective schools research. Much of the research was conducted in urban elementary schools, and many of the studies were very unique to the schools involved. There was a great dependence on test scores. Many of the researchers were not sure whether the characteristics identified were clearly the causes of instructional effectiveness. The factors have not been ranked. Although there is valid data on the factors related to school improvement, information is lacking about *how* and *why* change occurs. Experts are not really sure how an effective school became an effective school.

The literature clearly cautions educators against blindly accepting or attempting to institute all of the factors that apparently are associated with effective schools. There is no recipe for instant success.

Middle level educators must recognize not only the differences between elementary and secondary education but also the differences between elementary and middle school education. Moreover, as middle schools continue to create their unique identity, it will be easier to describe and assess the characteristics of an effective middle school.

In the meantime, leaders in middle level education should mesh the findings of the effective schools research with knowledge of the unique identity of the middle school as they delineate the characteristics of an effective middle school. In the next chapter, eleven characteristics of an effective middle school are described. These characteristics reflect both the results of effective schools research and the unique nature of early adolescents.

An effective middle school cannot be created overnight. Schools must begin to move in that direction; and, via incremental transition, take one step at a time in embracing the middle school concept. It is also essential to examine the change process to learn the potential pitfalls in making this transition. Middle schools must move from a highly departmental approach to an approach that reflects the developmental needs of students.

Teachers and principals share key roles in this change process. Teachers must recognize the potential of the middle school concept and take advantage of the opportunity to actively participate in the creation of a new or expanding program; they must show ownership for this program. As opportunities are presented, teachers must demonstrate leadership, and must learn to be flexible as they work to respond to the needs of early adolescent students.

Principals must orchestrate this faculty participation in implementing change, learn how to translate theory into practice, and overcome the obstacles to change. Throughout this entire process, principals must maintain commitment to the middle school concept. Building the master schedule is just the beginning of teaching the faculty how to implement the middle school concept. Principals can help teachers communicate effectively with each other. While managing the teachers' contract on a daily basis, the principal must work to invoke change as the middle school concept becomes a reality. The eleven characteristics will serve as a guide to the process.

Chapter II
Characteristics of an Effective Middle School

The cumulative literature of the middle school movement as well as the effective schools research serve as the basis of this set of eleven characteristics of an effective middle school. Part II of this publication describes processes which may be used to understand and implement each of these characteristics. The key to the successful implementation of all of these characteristics is the active involvement of teachers in the staff development process.

AN EFFECTIVE MIDDLE SCHOOL:

(1) FEATURES A PROGRAM THAT RESPONDS TO THE PHYSICAL, INTELLECTUAL, SOCIAL-EMOTIONAL AND MORAL NEEDS OF EARLY ADOLESCENTS.

Current data about the physical, intellectual, social-emotional, and moral development of the early adolescent must be examined. The earlier onset of puberty, the unevenness of growth, the cognitive development process, the importance of the peer group and self concept, the sensitivity of students, and the importance of values education need to be internalized. Then, educators should identify the implications of these data to realize the importance of counseling and guidance, the variety of activities needed within a lesson, the need to include concrete examples as concepts are introduced, the needed focus on skill development, the important role of peer tutors, the place of a home-base program, and the need for consistent discipline policies. Further, educators should identify and integrate the implications of the data from all of these categories to analyze the curriculum, school organization options, nature of the learning environment, reading program, and role of the classroom teacher. Specific aspects of the program must be based on identified needs of the student population.

(2) HAS A SET OF DOCUMENTS TO GUIDE ALL ASPECTS OF THE PROGRAM.

A number of key documents are needed to guide the development of the middle school program. There needs to be a clear definition of what a middle school is or ought to be. Once this definition is developed by the school district and/or the local school, it should be shared with the community.

A second critical document is a needs assessment which identifies the physical, intellectual, social-emotional, and moral needs of the students assigned to the school and places these needs in the context of the current school program. Pupil data to be included in a needs assessment are standardized test scores, achievement records, family history, interests, goals, and learning styles.

Thirdly, a philosophy and set of goals should be developed to reflect the overall direction of the school's program. Via a broad statement of philosophy and rather specific set of goals and objectives, the faculty and community can agree on their expectations of the program. This information may also be referred to as the mission statement of the school.

Finally, a rationale should be developed to give the underlying reasons for the major facets of the program. A rationale might include such subheadings as: interdisciplinary teams, grouping, curriculum, intramural program, and the home-base advisory program.

(3) POSSESSES A DEFINITE CURRICULUM PLAN THAT INCLUDES ORGANIZED KNOWLEDGE, SKILLS, AND PERSONAL DEVELOPMENT ACTIVITIES.

Alexander and others recommended a curriculum model that consists of factual information, skill development, and activities designed to help pupils understand and cope with the changes which they are or will be experiencing. Each course within the curriculum should feature these three elements. As teachers work together in the team planning process, efforts should be made to correlate content, skills, and personal development activities. Thus, this curriculum model becomes the basis of the team approach to instruction. The place of a home-base/advisory program in the curriculum must be addressed.

(4) HAS A CLEARLY ESTABLISHED PROGRAM OF STUDIES BASED UPON THE CONCEPT OF EXPLORATION AND PROVIDES OPPORTUNITIES FOR STUDENT GROWTH.

The program of studies should clearly reflect the needs of early adolescents. Courses that comprise the program for each grade level should reflect unique needs of students of that age. Certain subjects such as language arts and mathematics should be offered every year. Within the specific units of study for the course, evidence of growth and maturation should exist. Students need an opportunity to explore a great variety of areas such as music, industrial arts, or art rather than specializing via an elective program. In addition to the curricular experiences, pupils benefit greatly from an extensive co-curricular/activities/intramural program. Social-emotional needs of the early adolescent can be met via these aspects of the program. The goal is to develop a well rounded young adult; this can be best accomplished without an extensive electives program at this level.

(5) BUILDS ON THE STRENGTHS OF ELEMENTARY EDUCATION AND PREPARES STUDENTS FOR SUCCESS IN HIGH SCHOOL.

An effective middle school is a transitional experience for pupils who are at various stages of approaching adolescence. The program should build on the successes of elementary education by focusing on the learning needs of each student as an individual, having a sequential approach to skill development, providing for the correlation of content, and having a team approach to teaching. The teaching of reading and related communication skills should be emphasized in every subject area every period of the day.

In turn, the middle school experience should adequately prepare students for the ninth grade program in the high school where students will likely have various teachers in a fully departmentalized approach and have more decisions to make with regard to the curricular as well as the extracurricular program. The middle school should serve as a meaningful connection between elementary and high school education. Articulation activities are needed to ensure the greatest possible continuity between elementary and middle schools as well as middle schools and high schools. Articulation activities must include the active involvement of teachers and focus on the total scope and sequence of the K-12 curriculum. Pupils must be oriented as they move from the elementary to the middle school as well as from the middle school to the high school. Finally, students should be oriented to their unique opportunities at each grade level of the middle school experience.

(6) EMPLOYS TEACHERS WHO FOCUS ON THE LEARNING NEEDS OF PUPILS BY USING APPROPRIATE TEACHING STRATEGIES

Each middle school teacher should know the special learning needs of each pupil. Early adolescent students have diverse learning needs that are the result of their individualized timetable for physical, intellectual, social-emotional, and moral development. Appropriate techniques include student-to-student interaction; clear, concise structure for activities; adequate motivation, readiness, and goal-setting for each activity; clear transitions to connect the various activities; the inductive process; lessons that move from the concrete to the abstract; and enrichment activities for formal thinkers.

(7) CREATES TEACHING TEAMS USING BLOCK OF TIME TO BEST DELIVER THE INSTRUCTIONAL PROGRAM

Teaching teams provide an excellent opportunity to strengthen the instructional program, focus on the learning needs of pupils, and facilitate flexibility. Interdisciplinary teams usually consist of four or five teachers of four or five subjects who plan for and teach four or five classes during the same periods of the day. In grade six, two teachers could coordinate an interdisciplinary approach to the curriculum for a common group of students. A disciplinary team involves two or more teachers of the same subject who teach two or more classes of that subject at the same time. Block-of-time scheduling permits the teachers who teach at the same time to also be available for a common planning period.

Modular scheduling strategies permit teachers to subdivide the total block-of-time for teaching into various modules or time periods to accommodate all of the aspects of the instructional program. Teachers use a variety of team building activities to create a cohesive and unique identity for that team. The role and function of a team must be clearly delineated. Via inservice training, teachers may learn a number of team planning techniques to enhance the learning process for students.

(8) EMPHASIZES THE GUIDANCE AND COUNSELING FUNCTION OF STAFF MEMBERS BY PROVIDING FOR A HOME-BASE PROGRAM, STRESSING THE IMPORTANCE OF SELF-CONCEPT, AND PROVIDING A POSITIVE CLIMATE.

Every teacher in the building is, to a degree, a counselor by being sensitive to the needs of students. A student should be able to turn to any member of the professional staff with whom the student feels comfortable to seek help with a problem. Traditionally, secondary school teachers are responsible only for addressing the cognitive or informational needs of students. Middle school teachers, however, are asked to attend to the affective or emotional needs of a student's development.

The home-base or teacher advisory program may include orientation to the new school and/or grade, techniques to resolve conflict, study skills, and communication skills. All aspects of the instructional program should focus on the self-concept. The overall climate of the school should be positive so that youngsters will grow and learn in a healthy environment. A leadership team approach may be utilized to increase the sense of belonging on the part of the faculty.

(9) PROMOTES FLEXIBILITY IN IMPLEMENTING THE DAILY, WEEKLY, AND MONTHLY SCHEDULE TO MEET THE VARYING NEEDS OF STUDENTS.

Flexibility is a key word in the middle school concept. Since students are in a highly individualized stage of development, the schedule and program must be flexible in order to respond to changes and needs evident in the various stages of transition. The master schedule should provide the broad, general parameters but can and should be altered by the teaching teams on a daily, weekly, or monthly basis. Every class meeting need not be for fifty minutes. In some cases, classes can be less than fifty minutes; and, for specific purposes, classes could be extended to sixty or seventy minutes. On a weekly basis, special modules could be arranged for spelling, handwriting, or a skills lab program. Pupils could be grouped and regrouped as needed. Teaching sections within a team could rotate schedules, special arrangements could be made for field trips, or an entire team's schedule could be exchanged with another team's schedule on a semester or trimester basis.

(10) ACTIVELY INVOLVES PARENTS IN VARIOUS ASPECTS OF THE SCHOOL EXPERIENCE.

As in the elementary school, parents may play a key role in the learning experiences of middle school students. Schools must exert even greater efforts to make parents active participants, not just passive observers. Parents must learn about middle school curriculum and about the uniqueness of early adolescents. Parents may be called upon to volunteer their skills and expertise. Appropriate systems must be developed to help parents monitor the progress of their child in keeping with the need to provide children with greater opportunities for independence. Parents must be able to make the adjustments called for by the developmental tasks of early adolescence. The issues of dependence/independence, group identity, peer group pressures, and the search for sophistication require appropriate strategies for parents during these critical years of adjustment. Middle schools must make parents feel welcome and help parents realize that they are partners in the learning process.

(11) EVALUATES THE PROGRAM ON A REGULAR BASIS AND MAKES CHANGES THAT ENHANCE THE LEARNING.

Evaluation takes place in many ways. Surveys, questionnaires, feedback from parents, reports from regional accrediting groups, classroom observations, and the evaluations of individual teachers all provide important information which indicates if the program is succeeding. Those responsible for schools must monitor the extent to which learning is actually occurring and act accordingly. Goal-setting may emerge from the evaluative process and facilitate the improvement of the school's program. It is not necessary to wait until the end of the school year to make changes. Incremental transition is encouraged to facilitate a gradual implementation of the middle school concept and to dispel any notion that all aspects of the middle school program can or should be implemented at the same time.

Chapter III
The Change Process

The characteristics of an effective middle school can serve as guides for school improvement. This is true whether a school is making the initial transition to middle school, is in the process of expanding an existing program, is establishing long range goals, or when a group of teachers is interested in making program alterations. In each case, change is involved.

Prior to embarking on the broad topic of staff development to implement change, there must be a focus on the change process itself. Educational leaders must be fully aware of dynamics involved in creating change. Beyond writing goals and objectives, there must be a clear focus on how the people involved will be affected, will respond to the changes, and will ultimately facilitate the change process.

FULLAN'S MODEL FOR THE CHANGE PROCESS

In a review of the effective schools research, Michael Fullan (1985) focuses on the implications of these data in terms of change strategy. He sees change as a complex, dilemma-ridden, technical, socio-political process which may appear simple but in reality is complex. Fullan suggests a three part approach that may serve as an excellent paradigm for change to enhance the effectiveness of middle level education. The model has potential for those involved in the full actualization of the middle school concept as well as those focusing on one or two of the characteristics.

The three parts of the model are: (1) the psychological elements of a successful change process, (2) the limitations of the research in terms of the change process, and (3) alternative, complementary strategies or thoughts to achieve change. Practical examples related to middle schools are integrated with Fullan's model to provide a more comprehensive approach to the change process.

Despite the abundance of research on school improvement, there is little knowledge about *how* and *why* improvement occurs. Educators must realize that change is a process, not an event. Although more research is needed on how change occurs, it is obvious that individuals need to alter their ways of thinking and develop new skills for change to evolve.

The psychological elements of a successful change process include the following seven theses:

1. *Change takes place over time.* Change involves a number of factors that need to occur over a period of time. It is impossible for a school principal to mandate positive change. Sufficient lead time is needed to prepare a faculty for the transition to middle school or to implement the characteristics of an effective middle school. Even though teachers may be organized into interdisciplinary teams, the full implementation may take months or even years depending upon the degree to which the teachers are able to accept the teaming process as their mode for delivering instruction.

2. *The initial stages of any significant change always involve anxiety and uncertainty.* Teachers, students, parents, central office personnel, and school administrators are likely to be anxious about change. In planning for change, it is mandatory to deal with the affective issues of the change process. Although a factual base for the changes involved must be presented, there must also be adequate provision for people to release their apprehensions or anxieties. Those responsible for staff development programs must provide an opportunity for such a release in a developmental, accepting fashion.
3. *On-going technical assistance and psychological support assistance are crucial if the anxiety is to be coped with successfully.* Given the existence of anxiety as a reality, those responsible for program development must be able to train personnel in the skills required for success in instituting a new organizational system and also provide the necessary release for anxiety. Specific skills will be needed to help teachers function as members of a teaching team, develop and present a homebase or teacher advisory program, and/or teach a reading program involving a basal reader as a primary source. Time must be allocated to learn the skills, but time must be available to respond to the apprehensions of those receiving the technical assistance. The total inservice process must include both cognitive information and a release for anxieties.
4. *Change involves learning new skills through practice and feedback; it is incremental and developmental.* The technical assistance described must be presented to teachers, school administrators, and central office personnel using appropriate teaching techniques for adult learners. The learning process includes practice and feedback that reflects the concepts of mentoring and follow-up beyond the initial presentation. Staff development sessions must subdivide the content into sequential portions that reflect developmental learning for experienced professionals learning a new approach. Proper concern for the adult learner is a major factor in planning staff development.
5. *The most fundamental breakthrough occurs when people can cognitively understand the underlying conception and rationale with the respect to "why this new way works better."* Inservice training must provide an opportunity for teachers to cognitively comprehend the psychology of the early adolescent learner, the rationale for middle level curriculum, the organizational options for these grades, and the team process. The motivation to these sessions must include and support why the proposed approaches better meet the needs of the early adolescent learner. Teachers are more likely to implement change when they fully understand and can witness for themselves why the change is better for the student as well as the learning process.
6. *Organizational conditions make it more or less likely that the process will succeed.* Administrative leadership, both in the central office as well as the local school, is extremely important for change to occur. Administrative personnel need to believe in these changes

before they can expect teachers to implement them. Teachers will look at administrators as role models in this change process. Administrative personnel must make a commitment to understanding the middle school concept thoroughly before expecting staff members to do the same. The master schedule must provide an environment in which various aspects of the middle school program can grow and develop; thus, the reorganization of the master schedule is an essential early step.
7. *Successful change involves pressure through interaction with peers as well as administrative leaders.* Those teachers who are not fully committed to the middle school concept will need to feel pressure from others who are enthusiastic about the program. The peer pressure of those opposed to the change could deter the success of the change process if left unchecked. Administrators must work hard to insure that the peer pressure is positive, supportive, understanding, and nurturing. Change will occur when all staff members realize the commitment of the district and the principal to the successful implementation of the middle school concept.

Psychological factors play a very important role in the successful transformation to middle schools. Despite the weight of factual information, the affective aspects of individuals' reactions to the change are more likely to determine behavior. Leaders must clearly recognize the human factors of the implementation of the middle school concept, allow for the necessary release of anxieties, and move constructively toward successful program implementation.

Fullan's model also identifies some important limitations and points out that these limitations are further compounded by unsolvable problems, narrowness of goals, demographics, abstraction or misunderstanding, and transfer/sequencing problems.
1. *Unsolvable problems.* One example of an unsolvable problem is the number of periods per day that an interdisciplinary team can be responsible for a group of students. Within the allotted time, there may not be time for a regularly scheduled home-base program, sufficient time for reading skills development, or a special interest exploratory program. Another problem may be the number of periods available for team planning. Obviously, the greater the number of periods allotted, the more those teachers can accomplish. On the other hand, additional teachers might have to be hired to provide the desired number of team planning periods, and additional funds may not be available. The transition to middle school may also bring about the need for curriculum revision. A goal of the middle school is to teach children to think abstractly, but there may be limits to the levels that many children can reach. In short, there may well be some problems connected with the transition to middle school that will have serious impact on the implementation of the new program.
2. *Narrowness of goals.* A problem may arise considering the importance of goal-setting as a process and the importance of all goals. Ideally, goals should be broad such as the implementation of a home-base program or the teaching of reading in the content areas. Both of

these goals involve extensive staff development. As the list of goals expands, those responsible for goal-setting should clearly examine the interrelatedness of all goals to avoid a narrow focus on some of the goals.
3. *Demographics.* Much of the effective schools research is based on small samples of inner-city schools. Suburban communities must realize that the middle school concept is appropriate for all students, not just for minorities, inner-city youth, or students with learning disabilities. Those responsible for presenting the middle school concept to community groups must make these reports at the level of sophistication of the residents of a community. It is difficult to predict how given communities and different teacher populations will react to change. In some cases, it is easier to implement change in a small school than a large one.
4. *Abstraction/misunderstanding.* The middle school concept is an abstract concept for many. The principal must conceptualize the entire middle school concept and transition prior to leading the faculty through a series of concrete learning experiences. Systems are needed for frequent monitoring of program implementation and student progress during the time of transition. The role of the parents will need to be clarified in the middle school. Misunderstandings may arise when there is poor leadership within the building, poor leadership in the central office, or poor relationships between the teachers and the school board. Little is known about how effective schools became effective schools.

Little is known about the process of change because it is abstract for so many individuals. Factors that caused an effective middle school to become effective must be identified and studied in detail. It is also necessary to learn how the various factors influence each other. There is also very little research on schools that are *not* effective. Such abstractions and misunderstandings impact heavily on the change process.

5. *Transfer/sequencing.* It is not easy to gain an understanding of something in one setting and then implement it in another. It is not always easy to implement a district plan for the transition to middle school. Various individuals may sabotage the implementation plan. Teachers or leadership personnel may not have the necessary skills to implement the plan at the level expected by the district.

In addition to these five limitations, there is also the possibility that some of these factors will work in concert with others to impact upon a given situation. Change is a highly complex issue, and managing it involves balancing many factors.

The final portion of Fullan's model is actually a checklist of alternative, complementary strategies to achieve change.

    _____ 1. *Develop a plan.* An overall plan for a district as well as each individual school must be formulated at the outset of the project. Decisions have to be made on how progress toward implementing the plan will be monitored. Teachers and administrators must have input in creating that plan based on a study of the literature and the inductive process.

_____ 2. *Invest in local facilitators.* Outside consultants are important, but local facilitators are needed to implement the plans suggested by the visiting consultants. The local facilitators can help each school, and thus schools receive equal support throughout the transition process.

_____ 3. *Allocate resources.* Funds and time must be provided so that all staff personnel can attend workshops, institutes, and conferences prior to and during the early stages of program implementation. There must be sufficient lead time prior to the implementation for maximum preparations.

_____ 4. *Select schools and decide on scope of projects.* A district should probably begin with a pilot project. Program implementation should start small and grow. Whenever possible, participants in the pilot experiences should be volunteers. Incremental transition is highly recommended.

_____ 5. *Concentrate on developing the principal's leadership role.* The middle school setting provides an excellent environment for the principal to serve as an instructional leader. Training and support are needed, however, for the principal to learn and sustain the necessary skills. Assistant principals and prospective administrators must also receive similar training.

_____ 6. *Focus on instruction.* The bottom line in the effective middle school is children's learning. In addition to focusing on instructional issues, pupil services, and extracurricular activities, the emphasis on self-concept must be evident. Evidence of the existence of the middle school concept must be found in every classroom within the building, not just in the corridors or in the principal's office.

_____ 7. *Stress ongoing staff development and assistance.* Staff development is a continuous process. Staff development is needed for all aspects for the middle school program and must be geared to the needs of the staff. Technical assistance is needed.

_____ 8. *Plan for continuation and spread.* By gathering information and analyzing that information, future goals may be established. Schools must have the opportunity to share their successes with each other. Schools must also have the opportunity to analyze their problems in a cooperative, non-threatening atmosphere. In order for the program to continue and spread, there must be an open approach to evaluation.

_____ 9. *Review capacity for future change.* Change must be made gradually but must occur. Growth is evident in the changes implemented. There must be publicity for the evaluative process. Recognition should be given to those staff members who helped to achieve success.

Fullan's review of research of effective schools provides insights for the change process with definite implications for implementing effective middle schools. By analyzing the implications of the psychological elements of a successful change process, the limitations of the research in terms of the change process, and alternative strategies to achieve change, leaders in middle level education will be better prepared to design staff development programs that will facilitate effective middle schools.

COMBINING A DEPARTMENTAL AND DEVELOPMENTAL APPROACH

In a report on middle schools, James McPartland and his colleagues at the Center for Research on Elementary and Middle Schools at The Johns Hopkins University (1987) point out that some of the next steps for research in middle schools will be to help middle school resolve their unique dilemma—how to successfully balance the conflicting demands of promoting student growth and development and still focus on student learning. A significant aspect of the change process is to combine a departmental approach with the developmental approach to better focus on the learning needs of the early adolescent. Middle level schools are traditionally highly departmentalized. Effective middle schools must find ways to reduce departmentalization and build on the developmental approach in designing appropriate programs.

As the instructional leader, the principal should constantly work to help teachers operate within departmental structures to meet the developmental needs of early adolescents. This can be achieved by helping teachers understand the middle school concept—cognitively and affectively. Once this goal is achieved, teachers are ready to examine team structures such as the interdisciplinary, disciplinary, or core/combination approaches for improving the delivery of curriculum. Common planning periods must be provided if teams are to succeed.

Further, the principal can play a key role in providing inservice activities on the needs of early adolescent students. As teachers study the literature, they will be better prepared to become more caring adults and counselors for their students. Teachers will also be more accepting of appropriate teaching strategies for the early adolescent, models of grouping and regrouping students for instruction, and recognizing students for their accomplishments throughout the year.

Principals may also play a major role in goal-setting for professional growth. Goal-setting will focus on the climate of the school as well as the competencies of each staff member. As an instructional leader, the principal will play a key role in helping the faculty move from a highly departmentalized model to one that clearly responds to the needs of students while still retaining the essence of a departmentalized structure.

The change process is extremely complex, but unquestionably contains the key to the successful transformation to the middle school. The creation of effective middle schools reflects the importance of helping all of those who work in the school to learn what is expected of them in this new mode of organization.

Chapter IV
Staff Development

Staff development is an essential element in the successful implementation of the middle school concept. Effective middle school programs use a variety of staff development strategies. One of the keys to program development is faculty involvement. As faculty and staff become involved, successful implementation follows.

Staff development is the means by which the professionals in a school district learn how to implement new programs and grow professionally. As new programs emerge nationally or locally, teachers need to learn how to implement such programs. Central office as well as local school administrators should provide teachers with intense periods of study so they will understand these innovations.

When teachers know about a new program, they are better able to contribute to the design of the program. When they contribute to the design of the program, they feel more responsible for the success of the program. When teachers feel more responsible for the success of the program, programs are more successful.

School districts cannot turn to undergraduate schools to provide the needed cadre of teachers for newer programs nor can they depend on graduate programs to provide the needed training. Therefore, school districts have to provide teachers opportunities to grow professionally on the job via activities, attending conferences, and participating in professional improvement programs.

Staff development is more critical at the middle level because of the rapid growth in the number of schools adopting the middle school concept and the lack of appropriately prepared teachers. Without staff development, change has little chance to occur.

Successful staff development activities involve teachers in decision making, goal-setting, leadership activities, and an assessment of the process. Motivation and interest must be sustained by those responsible for staff development within the school or the district. The ultimate goal is faculty support through intrinsic motivation. The principal plays a major leadership role but needs to encourage leadership to emerge from the faculty. Finding ways to actively involve the faculty in all aspects of staff development enhances the probability of successful program implementation.

CHARACTERISTICS OF AN EFFECTIVE STAFF DEVELOPMENT PROGRAM

A successful staff development program at the middle level must be based on adult learning theory. Adults are the ones changing from one form of school organization to another. A major outcome is a change in the pattern of meanings, values, behaviors, and attitudes of teachers.

Participants in staff development programs must realize the need for change and be able to integrate the needed changes into their daily operating habits.

For adults, change is particularly complex because it involves the elimination of old patterns as well as the implementation of new ones. There is a definite risk of failure for adults participating in a staff development experience. Although those who attend these activities want to learn something new, they are fearful that they will be less successful in the future than in the past when less complex systems were in place. Self-concept is as an important an issue for the adult learner as it is for the early adolescent. Administrators and teachers should be actively involved in this learning process.

Feinman (1980) points out that adult learning experiences should be "minds on" as well as "hands on." Adult learners must learn how to learn from their own experiences. This process is called reflective analysis and involves bringing new meanings and relationships to a level of conscious awareness. New learning should be applied in real life situations.

Those responsible for staff development should plan activities that focus on the individual and are problem oriented. Wherever possible, adults should draw on their own experiences. They should study theory and research, observe demonstrations, and practice with feedback. Coaching for successful transfer and application as well as peer support groups are other key ingredients.

A successful staff development program at the middle level must include the following additional factors:

- **a thorough understanding of the middle school concept**

   The staff development program must enable administrators, teachers, parents, and the community to know what a middle school is, how the middle level program can and should respond to the needs of early adolescents, what school organizational options are, and how to help teachers work as members of a teaching team. With an understanding of these basics, the staff development program will help teachers achieve the real potential of the middle school concept.

- **definite goals, objectives, and an organizational plan**

   There needs to be a master plan for the implementation of the middle school concept that will enable those responsible to translate theory into practice. Definite goals and objectives are needed to guide the program. These can be re-evaluated at certain key points along the way as activities are assessed in relationship to goals pursued. Each facet of the organizational plan should fit in with the overall scheme. The curriculum must be meshed with learner objectives. Coaching should be used to insure successful transfer. The goals should meet individual needs and lead toward modified teacher behavior.

- **sufficient lead time prior to the implementation of the project**

   Ideally, a staff development program should begin a minimum of one year before the conversion to middle school to allow sufficient time for program development and orientation activities. Many school districts have utilized two full years of preparation so that teachers, parents,

students, and members of the community could be more deeply involved in the transition process.
- **a sustained, sequential, continuous effort**
    Staff development cannot consist of one inservice course prior to the opening of school, one workshop lead by an outside consultant, or one speech given by the president of the state organization for middle level schools. Each of these activities may be desirable, but staff development should provide a variety of activities on a continuous basis. Additional activities should be based upon an evaluation of earlier activities. Followup is essential.
- **a sensitivity to the needs of teachers**
    Just as classroom instruction should be based on the needs of students, the staff development program should be based on the needs of the participants. A formal assessment process may be utilized to identify those needs. Once needs are identified, appropriate and meaningful programs can be planned based on those needs as well as adult learning theory. A variety of resources should be utilized, and activities should be problem oriented. The peer support systems should be monitored for effectiveness. Programs can be modified according to feedback received from the participants. Again, the goal is to modify teacher behavior.
- **motivate participants**
    Participants must be confident that they can meet the challenge of the successful transition to middle school. While these individuals will benefit from staff development activities, they must function independently on a daily basis. Building on their own experiences and contributions, they will be doing something new that is perceived of as relevant and satisfying. Incentives should be provided for teachers to use the concepts learned.
- **learning environment should be positive, trusting, and safe**
    Those involved in staff development activities feel secure as learners. The environment should be cooperative, not competitive. Activities should be presented in such a way as to respect the dignity of each individual. Their physical comfort is also important. Lighting, seating, temperature, visibility of slides or other visuals, and appropriate audio levels must be assessed regularly.
- **active involvement of the participants**
    Participants should do more than view films, video tapes, or listen to lectures. The staff development curriculum must reflect the importance of the participants' active involvement and feature a number of hands-on activities. The target audience should be involved in all levels of preparation, implementation, and evaluation. Participants should especially be involved in planning the activities to match the inservice curriculum to the learners' objectives. Instructors should be aware of attention span limitations of the participants and provide examples whenever possible.
- **the provision to train new teachers assigned to the school**
    As new teachers are assigned to the school, provisions should be made to absorb them into the program and enable them to become contributing members of the faculty. Specific training modules should

be designed for these novices. Instructors should promote transfer and application on a regular basis.
- **strong leadership of the principal as well as leadership emerging from the faculty**

    Leadership is a shared responsibility between the principal and those participating in the staff development program. Strengths of various participants should be identified and utilized. Participants should feel administrative support throughout the learning process. Local resource personnel should be utilized where those individuals have demonstrated the necessary skills and expertise. At the district level, the emphasis is to achieve the successful implementation of the middle school concept in each building. At the local school level, the emphasis is to achieve a balanced implementation throughout every classroom in the building.
- **create a staff development resource center or a middle school resource center**

    Each district should have a center for staff development activities or a specific resource facility to enhance the successful transition to middle school. Each individual school should also have a room or an area of the building where materials are available to teachers on a regular basis. In addition to print and non-print materials, the center also becomes the location for professional discussions.
- **the opportunity to add new dimensions to the program**

    Every aspect of the model middle school program cannot be in place during the first year. Some components can be in place by year's end; other aspects will need to be developed over the next several years. Via the staff development program, participants will be able to contribute to the additions or refinements of the middle school experience for the students in that school or district. New aspects of the program should relate to assessed needs of students.

WHO IS RESPONSIBLE FOR THE STAFF DEVELOPMENT PROGRAM?

The school district has the ultimate responsibility for providing the necessary staff development for implementing effective middle schools. The district determines the philosophy, rationale, and other guidelines for middle grades education. The conversion to the middle school concept should, in essence, be a fundamental part of the comprehensive staff development program of the district. In most cases, the district plans the total spectrum of staff development activities. Frequently, the staff development coordinator for the district outlines the role of the district and the role of the local school.

Individual schools have a major responsibility in providing the staff development required in that building. In many ways, the principal serves as the head of the staff development program for that building. If the principal is truly the instructional leader of the school, the principal should be a key person in the areas of program implementation and staff development. The principal must have a general plan for staff development in that building, work with the faculty to review goals, and monitor the implementation process. Additionally, the principal should be available to meet with individual or small groups of teachers, parents, central office personnel, or Board of Education members who need to ventilate their concerns, receive support, or be given direction. The principal who can provide leadership, motivate staff members to actively contribute to the successful implementation of a middle school program, and handle the normal questions or concerns that are raised is well on the road to developing an effective middle school program.

Teachers, of course, have a major stake in the success of the program. Some of the specific responsibilities of the faculty are to recognize the real potential of the middle school program, work within the framework of the teaching contract to meet the needs of pupils, offer constructive suggestions through appropriate channels, consider the needs of pupils in determining the priorities of the program, and take advantage of the opportunities for active involvement in the development of the program.

Staff development is most effective when it is a shared responsibility between the school district and the individual school and, within the individual school, between the faculty and the administration. The staff development coordinator for the district can work with an advisory committee that has both teachers and administrators as members of that committee. In this way, the program can be responsive to the needs of the district as well as the needs of each middle school.

A PROCESS/CONTENT APPROACH TO STAFF DEVELOPMENT

A process/content approach is suggested for creating the staff development program to successfully implement the middle school concept. Process refers to the techniques, procedures, or strategies used to achieve a goal or objective within the staff development program. Process implies a particular method of doing something such as an inservice course, a summer workshop, or visits to other middle schools.

Content is simply defined as all of the subject matter or material contained in the staff development curriculum for the middle grades program. Topics would usually include a study of the development of early adolescents, models for curriculum, and organizational options.

It is probably impossible to determine whether the content or the process is more important in assessing the value of the staff development program. Participants must be actively involved in a variety of meaningful activities. At the same time, they must have the opportunity to secure the information or data underlying the concepts. In reality, it is the interaction of process and content that facilitates real learning on the part of those involved in the various aspects of the program.

Some Examples of Process Activities

Some examples of processes or staff development activities appropriate to the successful implementation of the middle school concept are:
(1) *Classroom observations and conferences*—As the principal and other members of the supervisory team observe teachers and hold individual conferences, they can assess the extent to which that teacher is implementing the program. This is an excellent time for an individual conference to help the teacher understand an aspect of the program or feel good about the role that teacher is playing in making the new program work.

(2) *Department meetings*—Disciplinary or single subject teams may use department meetings effectively for staff development purposes. Teachers involved in interdisciplinary teams also benefit from meeting with other teachers of the same subject.
(3) *Team planning meetings*—Teaching teams—interdisciplinary, disciplinary, or core/combination—have an excellent opportunity for professional growth when they meet on a regular basis.
(4) *Faculty meetings*—New ideas can be presented to the total faculty. Faculty meetings can be used for a variety of professional growth activities.
(5) *Department chairmen meetings*—The principal can meet with department heads on a regular basis. Additionally, all of the department heads of a specific subject for the school district can meet periodically.
(6) *Meetings with team leaders*—The principal should meet with all the team leaders in the school on a regular basis to insure good communication between teams.
(7) *Meetings with teams*—The principal should meet periodically with each of the teaching teams. These meetings provide the opportunity for the principal to see the personality of each team and to interact with individual teachers.
(8) *Inservice courses*—Organized courses should be available for teachers and other staff members to participate in indepth experiences relative to the middle school concept.
(9) *Attending conferences, conventions, institutes*—All professional personnel, including teachers, benefit greatly by attending workshops and meetings that focus on middle grades education.
(10) *Reading professional journals*—School districts and individual schools should subscribe to journals, newsletters, and other services that provide up-to-date information about early adolescent students and programs.
(11) *Guest speakers*—Experienced middle level educators can address a faculty or all of the teachers in a district about an important aspect of middle level education. These sessions are usually motivational; staff members can identify with both professors and practitioners. Appropriate follow-up activities should be planned.
(12) *Teacher representation on committees*—At both the district and local school levels, there are opportunities to involve staff members in committees that address professional concerns. Some are standing committees; others may be formed just to look at a specific problem.
(13) *Professional study days*—Workshops can be planned on days when students are not in school or are dismissed early so teachers can participate in staff development activities. Such days are usually built into the school calendar.
(14) *Summer curriculum workshops*—Curriculum guides can be written and—or pilot projects can be developed by involving teachers and other staff members in summer workshops. This is also an excellent way to develop the leadership needed for the middle school to be successful.

(15) *Graduate courses*—Colleges and universities offer courses that complement staff development programs. In many cases, teachers are reimbursed for taking courses that extend their professional competencies.

(16) *Visiting other schools*—Staff members can learn new information by visiting other middle schools that are in different stages of program implementation. Specific purposes should be established for these visits.

(17) *Membership in professional organizations*—Professional growth occurs as a result of the activities and resources made available to members by professional organizations that focus on middle grades education.

(18) *Mobile on-site training units*—A team of professionals can visit each school to teach teachers how to implement new programs and ideas. These teams can visit for several weeks during the school year.

(19) *Mentoring*—Mentoring is a process in which an experienced member of the faculty takes a direct, personal interest in the professional development of younger staff members or teachers who were recently assigned to the staff. The mentor becomes a role model to enable the protege to develop to maximum potential.

(20) *Peer coaching*—In peer coaching, some teachers assume responsibility for the professional growth of their colleagues. The goal of coaching is to insure that the training being received is being transferred to the classroom. To become a peer coach, one usually needs training in the related skills.

The list of processes for staff development is by no means exhaustive. Those responsible for staff development should think in terms of the tasks of implementing effective middle schools and how these tasks or activities can help to achieve that goal. These techniques should also be kept in mind while reading the next section on content.

Content Topics

A number of topics should comprise the content portion of the staff development program. The major topics are:

I. Characteristics of an Effective Middle School
II. Making the Transition to Middle School
III. The Early Adolescent Student
  A. Data about physical, intellectual, social-emotional, and moral development
  B. Implications for school organization, curriculum, role of the teacher, and nature of the learning environment
IV. Drafting Key Documents
  A. Defining the Middle School
  B. Conducting a Needs Assessment
  C. Writing the Philosophy, Goals, and Rationale
  D. Mission Statement
V. Implementing a Curriculum Model
  A. Organized Knowledge
  B. Skills
  C. Personal Development
VI. Organizational Options
  A. Interdisciplinary
  B. Disciplinary
  C. Core/Combination
VII. Role and Function of a Team
VIII. Team Building Activities
IX. Articulation with Elementary and High Schools
X. Building the Master Schedule
  A. Block-of-Time Approach
  B. Steps in Constructing the Schedule
XI. Flexible/Modular Scheduling
XII. Teaching Strategies for Early Adolescents
XIII. Grouping and Re-grouping Students for Instruction
XIV. Effective Use of Planning Periods
XV. Role of the Team Leader
XVI. Roles of Administrative/Supervisory Personnel
XVII. Evaluating the Program

Bringing Process and Content Together

The process and content factors need to be brought together at an appropriate point. For example, the content area may be "Teaching Strategies for Early Adolescents." Initially, it is necessary to differentiate an approach that may be taken at the district or local level. Secondly, it is helpful to identify processes that are intended to introduce the topic and other activities that will be used to reinforce the content or skills at some later stage. The introductory and reinforcement processes need to be carefully orchestrated.

Two examples of bringing process and content together are:

(1) Content: "Role of the Team Leader"
Level: School District
Introductory: 　　Summer workshop with consultant 　　Faculty meeting
Reinforcement: 　　Inservice course during fall semester 　　Meetings of team leaders at individual schools 　　Informal evaluation of team leaders at the end of the first semester
(2) Content: "Use of Flexible Scheduling Techniques"
Level: Local School
Introductory: 　　Guest speaker on professional study day 　　Faculty meeting—practicum experience for all faculty members
Reinforcement: 　　Discussion at meetings of team leaders and the building principal 　　Analysis of utilization of flexible scheduling practices conducted by the director of research

ESTABLISHING PRIORITIES AND TIMETABLE

A timeline should be developed for the purpose of implementing the middle level program and identifying persons responsible for specific aspects of implementation. Priorities are needed; those involved should begin work immediately on those items essential at the outset of the conversion process. The timetable then becomes a basis of evaluating the extent to which the program is being implemented.

The faculties of individual schools, the community, and central office personnel should have input in establishing priorities and determining the timetable. In this way, all who participate in programming the implementation can work cooperatively toward the goals which have been mutually established.

Priorities and a timetable are needed not only in the initial conversion to a middle school but also in the expansion of a program or the orientation of new staff members. Staff members should discuss such questions as:

1. What are our primary and secondary goals?
2. What are our immediate needs?
2. How can we adjust our list or priorities?

Dialogue and reflection on growth are needed in establishing priorities for the development of a timetable. Once developed, the timetable should be publicized to the community, taxpayers, parents, central office personnel, Board of Education members, and faculties. The timetable must be viewed, however, as subject to modification.

EVALUATING THE STAFF DEVELOPMENT PROGRAM

Thought needs to be given to the evaluation of the staff development program. Johnston and Markle (1979) suggested a process of structured questioning or interviewing to reach valid and reliable conclusions about the effectiveness of a program. They suggest this list as a general scope and sequence for a question-directed evaluation.

1. **What are we trying to evaluate?** Precisely what portion of the total middle grades education package are we trying to assess? Program evaluation will be more effective if specific components of the program can be identified. For example, it is more desirable to define the object of evaluation as the "inservice courses" than the "staff development program" or, the object of the evaluation can be "the use of the team planning period" rather than the "staff development program."
2. **What do we expect this program component to accomplish?** What are the specific objectives of the program? What do we expect teachers to do as a result of their participation in the program? For example, team planning periods might be expected to encourage teachers to focus more on the skill development processes as they plan their lessons. Also, team planning periods should help teachers focus more on the total learning needs of a student.
3. **What will we accept as indicators that the program is achieving its objectives?** Can we list the teacher behaviors that will allow us to conclude that the program element has had a desirable impact? Do teachers correlate topics in one subject with topics in other subjects? Do teachers on the team have a skill-of-the-week program?
4. **What sources of data are available which will indicate the presence or absence of the indicators?** What kinds of data on teacher behaviors do we already have? What kinds of data must be collected? Can structured observations of team activities be scheduled? Can teacher self-report data be utilized? In general, what kinds of data can be assessed in a reasonable period of time with a manageable effort?
5. **What specific information from each source will be most valuable to the program evaluation?** Within each data source, what information is most clearly related to the objectives of the program? How can this information be gathered, assembled, and organized?
6. **What do the data that we have collected state about the indicators?** Do the data state that the indicators are present or absent? What indicators are present that were not anticipated?
7. **Based on the presence or absence of indicators, what can be concluded about the effectiveness of the program?** Are the indicators of a process (inservice, team planning periods) present in sufficient numbers and strength to conclude that the program is working? Can the conclusion be justified on the basis of the data rather than personal opinion or the strength of one's desire for the program to succeed?

Although other approaches can be utilized, the model by Johnston and Markle can be used in assessing the effectiveness of elements of a staff development program.

In summary, a key to the successful implementation of middle schools is staff development. Responsibility for the staff development program should be shared between the central office and the local school. The principal plays a major role in implementing the staff development experience in that building. The interaction of process and content facilitates real learning on the part of those involved in the staff development activities. Staff development enables teachers to make a significant contribution to the development of the program.

Part II
Implementing Effective Middle Schools

Chapter V
A Model For Implementing the Characteristics of Effective Middle Schools

A plan for implementing effective middle schools should be based upon a systematic approach to achieving each of the eleven characteristics of an effective middle school. In this chapter, a specific plan will be presented to successfully implement each programmatic piece. The sequence for fulfilling the characteristics may be determined by the individual district or school. Schools or districts that have completed the initial transition to middle school may utilize one or more of these plans to improve or add a particular component.

The five facets of the implementation model are: (1) an understanding of the conceptual basis or theory described in the literature, (2) the leadership required from administrative/supervisory personnel, (3) opportunities for faculty participation, (4) the goal-setting process, and (5) assessment/evaluation.

UNDERSTANDING THE CONCEPTUAL BASIS OR THEORY DESCRIBED IN THE LITERATURE

To successfully implement a specific characteristic of an effective middle school, the process must begin with a full understanding of the conceptual basis for that characteristic. Since the early 1960's, the body of knowledge about middle level education has expanded greatly. New data about the developmental needs of early adolescents appear in the literature regularly. Descriptions of curriculum models for prepubescent and pubescent learners as well as organizational options for middle school can be readily located. Journals, monographs, textbooks, filmstrips, and videotapes are now available from various professional organizations and publishers. Conferences on middle level education are sponsored regularly by major education groups in various parts of the country.

Middle level educators have, for the past twenty-five years, adopted successful programs, techniques, and strategies derived from theory and put them into practice. Team organization, flexible schedules, and teacher advisory programs have emerged from an analysis of theory. This analysis of theory will help middle level educators develop both long and short range goals. As a result, there will be a further expansion of theory.

Sources such as the monographs published by the National Middle School Association should be consulted in the process of implementing the characteristics. Audio and video tapes available through the National Middle School Association, the Association for Supervision and Curriculum Development, and the National Association of Secondary School Principals are also important sources to use in gaining an understanding of the conceptual basis for many of the characteristics. Those responsible for the transition to middle school or the expansion of an existing middle level program must study the theory in the literature before attempting to put that theory into practice. Although each characteristic is significant, each can be established on its own merits but must also have a connection to the totality of the middle school concept.

LEADERSHIP FROM ADMINISTRATIVE/SUPERVISORY PERSONNEL

Ideally, leadership for the implementation of the characteristics should come from the central office. The superintendent should have a clear vision of the totality of the middle school concept and provide needed direction. Emerging from the central office should be an expressed commitment to implementing the full middle school program. Leadership roles of the members of the superintendent's staff as well as the various instructional supervisors should demonstrate a singular commitment to program development. Central office personnel should be extremely supportive of the change process, facets of program development, and staff development activities. One of the district's goals should be to achieve consistency in implementing the middle school concept throughout all of the middle schools in that district.

There should also be evidence of a close working relationship between the central office and the local school. Teachers in a given school should be able to identify which goals or priorities have been established in the central office and which have come from the local school. The staff development program, for example, should reflect the leadership of both the central office and the local school.

The building principal is a key person in providing administrative/supervisory support at the local school level. If the principal is truly the instructional leader of the school, the principal is a key person in program implementation and staff development. The real challenge is to create and motivate a staff development program that actively involves the total faculty.

The principal has two major functions in the process of implementing the characteristics of an effective middle school. First, the principal must be the overall leader of the implementation process. This includes having a general plan of direction, working with the faculty to review goals, and monitoring the implementation process. Secondly, the principal must be available to meet with individuals as well as small groups of teachers, parents, central office personnel, or Board of Education members who need to speak to the principal to express their concerns as well as to receive support or direction. The principal who can motivate staff members, actively contribute to the productive implementation process, and handle the normal questions or concerns that are raised is well on the road to developing an effective middle school program.

In addition, assistant principals, department heads, house coordinators, and team leaders should play major roles in staff development. There should be an obvious connection between the efforts of the local school and the central office. The goal is to provide the needed support for teachers to make changes.

An example of leadership from administrative/supervisory personnel could be the institution of a careful analysis of curriculum to determine the extent to which the curriculum responds to the physical, intellectual, social-emotional, and moral needs of the early adolescent learner. Administrative/supervisory leadership should also be evident in the development and dissemination of basic documents, the development of an appropriate program of studies to facilitate the concept of exploration, and the staffing guidelines needed for a team teaching program utilizing a block-of-time base.

OPPORTUNITIES FOR FACULTY PARTICIPATION

A successful model for implementing the characteristics of an effective middle school must include ample opportunities for faculty participation. Teachers are the ones most able to identify topics to be correlated within the curriculum plan, suggest skills to be included in the skill-of-the-week program, or write units of instruction for the home-base program. Teachers should have a major role in developing the extra-curricular program and in finding ways to improve the needed articulation between the elementary and the middle school programs.

The master schedule can be created by a committee that consists of teachers and administrators. This committee can help to train teachers in modular scheduling techniques to effectively meet the learning needs of early adolescent students. Teachers can also help to identify strategies to actively involve parents in various aspects of the learning process as well as to participate in the evaluation of the middle school program.

As the school district or school starts the process of learning about the middle school concept, teachers should be involved extensively. Teachers should attend conferences, visit other middle schools, serve on various committees, develop position papers, conduct parent information sessions, and help to orient other teachers and students. From an instructional viewpoint, teachers will discover the real potential of the middle school concept as they participate in program implementation.

Teachers must also play an important part in decision-making at both the district and local school levels. In addition to committee opportunities, certain decisions should be relegated to local school faculty committees, the various teaching teams, or the various departments of instruction.

Like students, teachers learn best via a hands-on approach. Inductive strategies should be encouraged as teachers explore new information and offer suggestions in the decision-making process. Pilot projects should emerge from these exploratory experiences. Those who have had the benefit of participating in pilot projects or who have benefitted from special training should conduct staff development for other teachers. Mentoring and peer coaching provide excellent opportunities for faculty participation.

As teachers become knowledgeable, proficient, and actively assist in educating others, a sense of ownership in the program will be created. This perception of ownership is clearly the ultimate goal for faculty participation in the process of implementing a specific characteristic or the total program. When teachers make statements such as:

"This program belongs to us!"

"As we implemented the middle school program, we were treated like real professionals!"

"We will do what is necessary to make this program successful!"

"This program was not handed down from the central office; it is ours!"

it is evident that teachers are assuming ownership for the new program. As the evaluation process occurs, teachers will then be ready for commendations as well as constructive suggestions.

In summary, teachers must be given the opportunity to recognize the real potential of the middle school program, offer constructive suggestions through appropriate channels, consider the needs of pupils in determining the priorities of the program, and take advantage of opportunities for active involvement in developing the middle school program.

GOAL-SETTING

Goal-setting is a process of establishing priorities. Priorities are indicators of the path of the professional development desired. The goal-setting process may be closely connected to the appraisal process in that identified needs can then become the aspirations for the forthcoming year.

In implementing the characteristics of effective middle schools, the goal-setting process may help to establish the breadth and depth of the pursuit. A school district may establish the following goals for a given school year:

1) The school district will participate in a program to analyze the extent to which the seventh grade curriculum responds to the physical, intellectual, social-emotional, and moral needs of the early adolescent learner.

2) A district-wide committee will draft a philosophy statement for middle level education. The committee will consist of representatives of each middle school who will then help each school to design its philosophy statement to be congruent with the district statement and yet meet the unique needs of students in that building.

3) Teachers will implement a skill-of-the-week program coordinated by interdisciplinary teams.
4) A committee will be established to write and implement a homebase program for grades six and seven.

Based upon district-wide goals, each middle school may create its own goals and priorities. In some cases, these goals will reflect district-wide issues; in other cases, the unique needs of the school are recognized. Examples of school goals are:

1) Teachers of art, music, physical education, technology education, home economics, and foreign language will form exploratory teams. These teams will be scheduled for team planning periods comparable to the allocation for the interdisciplinary teams.
2) Teachers will study the demographics of the school population and identify special programs needed to assist students assigned to that school.
3) A committee will be formed to analyze the schedule building process to identify additional opportunities for flexible, modular scheduling.
4) A staff development team will be created to implement the writing-across-the-curriculum program.

Once the school goals are established, departments of instruction as well as teaching teams should meet to initiate their priorities for the year. Examples of departmental goals are:

1) The English department will play a leadership role in implementing the writing-across-the-curriculum program.
2) The mathematics department will analyze the performance of the students on the standardized mathematics tests to identify areas of weakness and a procedure for remediation utilizing a skills laboratory approach.
3) The guidance department will assume leadership responsibilities in creating the home-base program.
4) The social studies department will continue its efforts to identify opportunities within the curriculum to implement the values education curriculum.

Teaching teams should identify goals that reflect the needs of students at key intervals during the course of the year.
Examples of team goals are:

1) For the month of September, the team will teach and reinforce a manuscript form to be followed consistently by all teachers on the team.
2) Teachers will work together to correlate content.
3) At the end of the first semester, the team will identify students who are in danger of failing for the year and then work to identify their unique needs.
4) On the last day of school, the team will give awards to students on the team who have demonstrated the various aspects of the values program stressed by the team during the course of the school year. Time in the team planning periods will be devoted to identifying all the students who qualify within each category.

Finally, each individual teacher will list his or her personal goals for the school year. These goals may reflect the teacher's commitment to the school, department, team, or district. Additionally, the goals may reflect suggestions offered previously during the appraisal process or personal expectations for the school year. Thus, the district, school, department, team, and individual teacher have numerous opportunities to work toward the implementation of a particular characteristic of an effective middle school as well as the totality of the transition to middle school.

ASSESSMENT/EVALUATION

The final phase, assessment/evaluation, presents an opportunity to closely examine one particular aspect of the middle school concept or the overall effort to implement a true middle school. Where goals have been established, those involved can list what was accomplished toward the attainment of each goal. Rather than a qualitative statement about attaining the goal, the emphasis should be on the enumeration of accomplishments. For example, in working to create the home-base program, the guidance department organized a committee consisting of representatives of each department and teaching team, visited three neighboring middle schools to observe the home-base program, obtained copies of the home-base curriculum guides from ten schools in various parts of the nation, read and discussed *Adviser-Advisee Programs: Why, What, and How* (James, 1986), identified two potential organizational models for their school, and made a comprehensive presentation to the total faculty in preparation for initiating the home-base program for the next September.

The assessment/evaluation for each characteristic should not replace an overall, major evaluation conducted by individual school systems or the regional accrediting association. In assessing or evaluating a particular facet of the middle school concept, the emphasis should be on the singular consideration of that particular programmatic piece.

As the evaluation process occurs, recognition should be given to those individuals primarily responsible for the successes at the team, department, school, and/or district levels. A variety of media should be used in bringing such recognition. On the other hand, when shortcomings have been identified, constructive suggestions should be offered for improvement. The community should be aware of those aspects needing further attention. Teachers and administrators must receive positive direction for ameliorating concerns.

Throughout the assessment/evaluation process, all involved in implementing the middle school concept must maintain a commitment to the early adolescent student and the middle school concept. At times, it might be easier to abandon the middle school concept or some aspect of it. The professional response, however, is to find an appropriate way to continue the improvement effort.

SUMMARY

In this chapter, a model for implementing effective middle schools has been presented. The five facets of the model are: (1) an understanding of the conceptual basis or theory described in the literature, (2) the leadership required from administrative/supervisory personnel, (3) opportunities for faculty participation, (4) the goal-setting process, and (5) assessment/evaluation. In the remaining chapters, each of the eleven characteristics of an effective middle school will be presented. Following a brief review of the conceptual basis described in the literature, a series of activities will be presented. For each of these activities, questions will be included to elicit the needed leadership required from administrative/supervisory personnel, the active involvement of teachers in implementing the characteristics, a consistent approach to goal-setting, and the needed structure for assessment/evaluation.

Chapter VI

An Effective Middle School...

**Features A Program That Responds To The
Physical, Intellectual, Social-Emotional, And Moral
Needs Of Early Adolescents**

Within the past thirty years, extensive information about the early adolescent youngster has emerged. Middle school educators have a responsibility to review this literature and, more importantly, to use these data in developing programs that will respond to these needs.

Some would suggest that this characteristic of an effective middle school is the most important one and that other characteristics are merely extensions or applications of this factor. Further, because of the varying rates of development, the middle school program must respond to both the gross transition of all pupils and yet recognize that individual youngsters are going through this process at different rates and at different times. Specific middle school programs must be based upon and related to the learning and developmental needs of this age group. To develop such programs, educators should study the physical, intellectual, social-emotional, and moral needs of students.

This chapter will present in summary fashion information on each of these developmental categories. Models will be presented for a school system, an individual school, or a specific faculty group to use in studying the literature, identifying the implications of each area of development, and assessing the significance of the data for curriculum, school organization, nature of the learning environment, role of the middle school teacher, and/or the reading program. A series of activities that will facilitate an intensive study of the topic concludes the chapter.

PHYSICAL DEVELOPMENT

J. M. Tanner, a London pediatrician, noted the earlier onset of puberty and began a serious study of this occurrence. His research produced data to show that the whole process of growth had been progressively speeded up and that children born in the 1930's or the 1950's matured earlier and were considerably larger than those born in the 1900's. This phenomenon had a major bearing on the middle school movement.

Marked changes occur at the onset of puberty, though boys and girls follow a somewhat different blueprint. For girls, this growth tends to occur between the ages of 12 and 12½; for boys, 14 to 14½. Growth is uneven; there are early and late maturers among both girls and boys. Thus, individual differences and variations in growth patterns are greatest among students at the middle school level. A significant study of the physical development of the transescent was the Boyce Medical Study conducted by Dr. Allen Drash and Dr. Donald Eichhorn. This research project looked at the variation in development and the impact of biological maturation on the learning process. A high correlation between learning and maturation was evident.

INTELLECTUAL DEVELOPMENT

There is also a wide range of mental development occurring between the ages of 10 to 14. One of the most exciting aspects of the entire middle school movement may be the recent discoveries in the areas of intellectual development and brain growth periodization.

Piaget's work was important in understanding how children grow in the area of cognitive development. He described the period of concrete operations between the ages of 7 and 11 that was followed by the period of formal operations beginning at approximately age 11 and continuing to age 15. During this latter period, the student begins to hypothesize and use logic while still having some difficulty with concepts such as government or photosynthesis.

The discoveries of Professors Epstein and Toepfer in the area of brain growth periodization not only have substantiated Piaget's thinking from a biological perspective but have provided even further insight into the early adolescent's intellectual processes and how they relate to curriculum. Dr. Epstein discovered that the human brain experienced growth spurts at certain times with virtually no growth at other times.

Probably the best known application of the work of Piaget and Epstein is the Cognitive Levels Matching Project at the Shoreham-Wading River (New York) Middle School. In *Cognitive Matched Instruction In Action*, Esther Fusco and her associates (1987) described efforts of teachers to become sensitive to child development. Teachers assessed the developmental levels of students and also evaluated the requirements implicit in curricular tasks. They received extensive training in order to make the necessary adaptations of methods and materials. As a result, teachers became adept in adjusting the appropriateness of curriculum to the developmental stages of the students. Learning, as a result, was enhanced.

SOCIAL-EMOTIONAL DEVELOPMENT

Middle school educators cannot be effective if they fail to recognize the social-emotional developmental problems of the early adolescent. The youngster becomes very sensitive about the body changes that have or have not taken place. The transescent needs help in controlling the related emotions. Achievement in school may be blocked by emotional disorganization. Aspects of the social-emotional development of the early adolescent include: (1) group membership, (2) self-concept, (3) ethnic identification process, (4) sex role identification, (5) peer approval, (6) independence from adults, and (7) a search for sophistication.

MORAL DEVELOPMENT

Adults want their children to have instruction in moral behavior, although some may disagree over what is taught or how it is taught. School systems across the nation are becoming more and more involved in moral development or values education programs.

The work of the late Dr. Lawrence Kohlberg of Harvard serves as the foundation for many of these programs. Kohlberg, using the term *moral reasoning,* suggested that teachers use moral dilemmas with their students. Kohlberg's work is considered cognitive moral development. The term *cognitive* stresses organized thought processes, the term *moral* involves decision-making in situations where unusual values come in conflict, and *development* suggests that patterns of thinking about moral issues improve qualitatively over time. Research in this area is still in the beginning stages. Unfortunately, the link between reasoning morally and acting morally is weak.

The Baltimore County, Maryland Public Schools embarked upon a program of values education based on the theme "1984 and Beyond: A Reaffirmation of Values." As a part of this project, the school system identified ten premises regarding values education. These premises are:

1. Values education needs to be defined.

2. There should be recognition that a common core of values exists within our pluralistic society.

3. There should be an awareness of the existence of conflicts among acceptable values.

4. There should be a greater awareness by teachers and administrators of the potential role of values in education and of their part in transmitting values.

5. Educators should be aware that values are taught implicitly and explicitly through the curriculum and by practices throughout the school system.

6. Educators should be aware of the values and ethics perspectives of the community as expressed by representatives of the public and private sectors.

7. Educators should understand that society supports an increasingly important role for the public schools in values education.

8. Knowledge gained from research in the field of values education and the developmental stages of children and youth should be applied to our approach to the topic.

9. Goals for the outcome of values education in terms of student behavior and character development should be established.

10. A recognized philosophy of values education and commitment to its implementation should be adopted by the school system and communicated to all related groups.

It is possible, according to the Baltimore County model, to identify a series of values to be incorporated into an educational program. The following values comprise the common core of values for a school or school district:

Compassion	Objectivity
Courtesy	Order
Critical Inquiry	Patriotism
Due Process	Rational Consent
Equality of Opportunity	Reasoned Argument
Freedom of Thought and Action	Respect for Others' Rights
Honesty	Responsibility
Human Worth and Dignity	Responsible Citizenship
Integrity	Rule of Law
Justice	Self-respect
Loyalty	Tolerance
Knowledge	Truth

The middle school organizational plan offers a unique approach to teaching moral development, values education topics, or the common core of values. On the one hand, most topics can be taught through the various subject areas in the context of existing curriculum. On the other hand, certain topics can be approached through the homebase or teacher/advisory program. Ideally, the interaction of teaching in content areas and the discussions in the homebase area reinforce one another. As students recognize that these topics have importance throughout the school, they will integrate or assimilate this information more readily.

USING THE DATA

The current middle school movement is, in many ways, a response to the growing awareness of the needs of early adolescents. Gathering information about the physical, intellectual, social-emotional, and moral development of early adolescents is just the first step in the process. As the second step, teachers should be actively involved in a discovery process to find the implications of these data for program development.

In chapter V, a model was suggested for implementing the characteristics of effective middle schools. The first segment of the model involved understanding the conceptual basis or theory described in the literature. This chapter featured an introduction to that material. The bibliography contains other references to be consulted. The other elements in the model were leadership from administrative/supervisory personnel, opportunities for faculty participation, goal-setting, and assessment/evaluation.

The next segment of this chapter features a plethora of activities to achieve, illustrate, and/or extend the first characteristic of an effective middle school. For each of these activities at the end of this chapter, the following questions should be asked:
- What leadership is needed from the central office to insure that the program responds to the needs of students?
- What strategies should the principal utilize to effectively supervise program implementation and development so that the program responds to the needs of the early adolescent?

- What opportunities are there for faculty participation in developing a program that responds to the needs of early adolescent students?
- How can the faculty effort be properly evaluated?
- What goals may be established by the district, the school, a department, or a teaching team so that the instructional program will consistently respond to the learning needs of students?
- What evaluative procedures would help in assessing the extent to which this characteristic is in effect?

ACTIVITIES

Using the information in this chapter as well as other resources available, teachers and other local school personnel should complete the following activities related to the first characteristic of an effective middle school. As a result of completing these activities, there should be sufficient indicators that the program responds to the physical, intellectual, social-emotional, and moral needs of the early adolescent learner. These activities may be conducted on a district-wide or on an individual school basis.

Activity #1:

Using the information in this chapter as well as other sources, teachers should list eight characteristics for each major subdivision of the needs of the early adolescent.

RESPONDING TO THE NEEDS OF THE EARLY ADOLESCENT LEARNER

I. **Characteristics**
 A. **Physical**
   1.
   2.
   3.
   4.
   5.
   6.
   7.
   8.

 B. **Intellectual**
   1.
   2.
   3.
   4.
   5.
   6.
   7.
   8.

C. Social-Emotional
   1.
   2.
   3.
   4.
   5.
   6.
   7.
   8.

D. Moral
   1.
   2.
   3.
   4.
   5.
   6.
   7.
   8.

Activity #2:

A key to the success of the middle school movement is the ability to identify educational implications of early adolescent characteristics. For each category of characteristics, teachers should identify five significant implications. An implication is what can or should be done in the middle school in response to the developmental characteristics.

II. Implications of Each Area
   A. Physical
      1. Students need a variety of activities within a class period because of their attention span limitations.
      2.
      3.
      4.
      5.

   B. Intellectual
      1. Teachers should use concrete examples in concept development.
      2.
      3.
      4.
      5.

   C. Social-Emotional
      1. The exploratory program should be a vital part of the curriculum for each grade.
      2.
      3.
      4.
      5.

D. **Moral**
      1. Teachers should find opportunities within each content area to teach the common core of values in the context of that content area.
      2.
      3.
      4.
      5.

   Activity #3:

   After identifying implications for each of the four areas of development, teachers are now ready to look again in a multi-disciplinary fashion at all of the areas to identify major implications for middle school curriculum, the organization of the middle school, the nature of the learning environment in the middle school, the role of the middle school teacher, and the reading program in grades 6, 7, and 8.

III. **Overall Implications of All Areas**
   A. **Curriculum**
      1.
      2.
      3.
      4.
      5.

   B. **Organization of the School**
      1.
      2.
      3.
      4.
      5.

   C. **Nature of the Learning Environment**
      1.
      2.
      3.
      4.
      5.

   D. **Role of the Middle School Teacher**
      1.
      2.
      3.
      4.
      5.

   E. **Reading Program for the Middle School**
      1.
      2.
      3.
      4.
      5.

Activity #4:

The middle school curriculum should respond to the needs of the early adolescent student. Toward this end, there should be topics in the curriculum for grades 6, 7, and/or 8 that reflect physical, intellectual, social-emotional, and moral development. The topics could become a part of the factual information in subject areas, a skills development program, and/or the home-base or teacher/advisory program at one or more grade levels. At this point, the focus is on topic selection; teachers and administrators should list potential topics for inclusion in the middle school curriculum responding to the needs and interests of this age group. Topics to be included are:

A. PHYSICAL DEVELOPMENT
  1. Physical Growth
  2. Growth Trends
  3. Sexual Development
  4. Emotional and Social Implications of Maturation
  5.
  6.
  7.
  8.
  9.
  10.

B. INTELLECTUAL DEVELOPMENT
  1. The Learning Process
  2. Study Skills
  3. Career Development
  4. Course Selection for the Next Grade
  5.
  6.
  7.
  8.
  9.
  10.

C. SOCIAL-EMOTIONAL DEVELOPMENT
  1. The Family and the Early Adolescent
  2. The School Environment
  3. The Community and the Early Adolescent
  4. Decision-Making
  5. Resolving Conflict
  6. Group Membership
  7.
  8.
  9.
  10.

D. MORAL DEVELOPMENT
   1. Expectations of Society
   2. Human Worth and Dignity
   3. Helping the Handicapped
   4.
   5.
   6.
   7.
   8.
   9.
   10.

Activity #5:

The Boyce Medical Study suggested an ungraded or developmental age grouping approach to organizing the middle school. The rationale for this approach was that students of the same chronological age are really at various maturational levels; thus, it may be more appropriate to group students by maturational levels than by chronological age. In this model, curriculum can then be differentiated according to maturational level and other factors affecting learning.
1. What opportunities exist for an ungraded approach in physical education, reading, art, band, chorus, and mathematics in your school or school district?
2. What opportunities exist for an ungraded approach for other content areas within your program of studies?
3. What are the advantages and limitations of using the ungraded approach in your school district or school?
4. What organizational changes are needed to facilitate ungraded instruction in your school or school district?

Activity #6:

Perhaps, your school or school district would become involved in a research program based upon the physical development of the students in your building. In addition to monitoring physical growth of individual students, these data could then be correlated with other significant information about the individual educational progress of individual students.
1. Develop a process to record the height, weight, blood pressure, pulse rate, and onset of sexual characteristics of individual students.
2. Create a process to correlate these data with achievement grades by marking period in each subject area, standardized achievement test scores, a self-assessment survey, and/or referrals from teachers to the office.
3. Study these data to look for norms, trends, and expectations for teachers and parents. The results may also be helpful to students to compare their growth and performance in the middle grades to other students.

Activity #7:

The program of student awards in the middle school should do more than recognize the outstanding athletes and the class valedictorian. Interdisciplinary teams or a committee of teachers on a schoolwide basis should create categories for the recognition of students. This acknowledgment should reflect variances in student growth and development, the totality of the curricular spectrum, and all factors involved in the learning process for early adolescent students.

The following categories are suggested as a beginning point in developing a program of student recognition that is consistent with growth patterns and the learning process of middle level students:

1. Achievement in each academic area
2. Effort in each academic area
3. Homework completed in each academic area
4. Improvement in each academic area
5. Accomplishment in each aspect of the physical education and/or intramural program
6. Citizenship
7. Elements of the Values Education Program
8. Attendance
9. Punctuality
10. Cooperation with students and teachers

Obviously, other categories can and should be added according to the school's goals, the uniqueness of students, and the priorities of the faculty. The ultimate goal is to recognize as many students as possible for their unique accomplishments during the middle school experience.

Chapter VII
An Effective Middle School...

**Has A Set Of Key Documents To Guide All
Aspects Of The Program**

Early in the process of developing a middle school, a number of key documents are needed. First, there should be a clear definition of a middle school developed by the school district or the faculty and shared with the community. Secondly, a needs assessment should be conducted as the basis for identifying the developmental needs of the students assigned to the school and to give direction to the improvement program. Thirdly, a philosophy and a set of goals should be developed to reflect the overall direction of the program of the district or individual school. Via a broad statement of philosophy and a rather specific set of goals or objectives, the school and community can agree on their expectations of the program. Finally, a rationale should be developed to give the underlying reasons for the major facets of the program.

The importance of drafting these key documents cannot be overemphasized. It behooves a school to be rather precise in defining the parameters of the middle school experience it wishes to provide for its students. More specifically, these documents are needed for the following reasons:

1. Each individual faculty should provide an exact definition of the term middle school which it is then ready to support.
2. To be fully effective, the curriculum must be geared to the assessed needs of the pupils.
3. The rationale for major decisions in the organization of the school should be known to all in the school and the community.
4. The evaluation of the school should be based on the basic documents described so the evaluation can measure the extent to which the school's objectives are being fulfilled.
5. Parents and community leaders should know the content of these major documents.

DEFINING A MIDDLE SCHOOL

Each faculty or local educational agency needs to develop a definition of the term middle school. Rather than accept an already developed definition, the teachers and staff should define the specifics of their perception of the middle school experience to be provided for their students.

At first, teachers might analyze and react to some definitions in the literature. Three samples are offered:

> 1. A middle school is an educational institution established to serve young people who are in the transition period between childhood and adolescence, most commonly composed of grades 6-8.
>
> Dr. John Lounsbury,
> Georgia College
>
> 2. The emergent middle school is a school providing a program planned for a range of older children, preadolescents, and early adolescents that builds upon the elementary school program for earlier childhood and in turn is built upon by the high school's program for adolescence. It is a phase and program of schooling, bridging but differing from the childhood and adolescent phases and programs.
>
> Dr. William Alexander,
> University of Florida
>
> 3. The middle school is that educational institution encompassing children ordinarily included in grades 6, 7, and 8 that is specifically designed in its operations to meet the needs of early adolescents.
>
> Dr. Robert McCarthy

Eventually, the faculty should develop a definition that might include the answers to questions such as:

Content:
1. What grades should be included?
2. What does the faculty want to accomplish as a middle school that they didn't as a junior high school?
3. What is to be unique about this school?
4. How might the following items or factors be reflected in the middle school program?
   a. continuous progress
   b. flexible schedule
   c. social experiences
   d. team planning and/or teaching
   e. balanced curriculum
   f. appropriate teaching strategies
   g. exploratory experiences
   h. teaching basic skills
   i. adolescent growth and development
   j. guidance and counseling
   k. positive school climate

Process:
1. Does the definition reflect a practical application of middle school theory?
2. What is the role of administrative/supervisory personnel in developing a definition?
3. How can teachers be involved in developing a definition?
4. How will the definition serve as a basis of the goal-setting process?
5. How will this effort be evaluated?

Each school district or school should develop its own definition early in the process of converting to the middle school plan; and, this definition can be revised or altered as the program becomes more complex. Those composing this definition should keep in mind the major purposes of the middle school as well as the uniqueness of the learning experience.

CONDUCTING A NEEDS ASSESSMENT

A needs assessment involves the acquisition of a picture of the middle school students enrolled in a particular school. Data to be included in a needs assessment are standardized test scores, achievement records, family history, interests of students, goals of students, learning styles of students, and sociological data. This data should be evaluated and synthesized to guide the direction of the instructional program so that pupil needs are met.

Those charged with conducting the needs assessment should look at the parameters of the total group and the individual differences that exist within the group. Consistent with the concepts of transition and difference, those gathering data must be able to make decisions reflecting the sum total of the data as well as the important factors needed for placement of individuals within the overall group. This information can be gathered by reviewing student records, talking with teachers at the feeder elementary schools, studying surveys, and interviewing a sampling of students and their parents.

A cycle is suggested in developing a needs assessment. The first phase of the cycle is a gathering of the data followed by a careful analysis of the needs evident from a review these data. Those responsible for program development must then plan a middle school curriculum that responds to pupils' needs. The final stage is evaluating the success of the plan and/or the periodic up-dating of the assessment data.

Faculty groups can determine the kinds of information to be gathered as well as possible uses of the needs assessment. The leadership of administrative/supervisory personnel in this project is vital. Some samples of the kinds of charts or graphs to be developed are:
1. An analysis of reading scores. There must be a careful analysis of the results of standardized test data, results of informal reading inventories, and an analysis of teacher assessment of reading progress. These data can be analyzed in terms of non-verbal IQ scores.
2. An analysis of mathematics scores. There must be a careful analysis of standardized test data as well as an analysis of teacher assessment of progress in mathematics These data can also be analyzed in terms of non-verbal IQ scores.
3. An analysis of nonverbal intelligence test scores in isolation.
4. An analysis of the results of standardized language arts tests.
5. An analysis of enrollment patterns within the school or the school system.

PHILOSOPHY AND GOALS

Philosophy is generally defined as a science which investigates or delineates the facts and principles of a particular situation or environment.

Goals, on the other hand, are the marks to be set or the end which a design tries to approach. *Middle School/Junior High School Evaluative Criteria,* developed by the National Study of School Evaluation, suggests that a school program should be developed in terms of what is striving to develop—its philosophy and goals statement.

A number of suggestions are offered to a faculty group in developing a philosophy and set of goals:

1. List the important factors to be included in the philosophy and listing of goals.
2. Identify how the philosophy will reflect both the nature of the school system and the individuality of the local school.
3. Determine how this statement should guide the instructional process.
4. Give examples of how the roles of the professional staff shall be determined by the philosophy.
5. State how the child in this environment will learn and be evaluated.
6. Separate the major from the lesser goals.
7. Plan an orientation for the community so they may initially provide input and eventually be familiar with the documents produced.

The following philosophy and goals statement appears as an example. Those involved in writing a similar document might benefit from examination of this example but should by no means feel compelled to reproduce it for another school situation.

> We, the faculty, commit ourselves to the middle school as an institution in which students may achieve mastery of basic skills and acquire basic knowledge necessary to develop a positive self-image and to foster academic, social, and personal growth. We obligate ourselves to identify and meet the diverse needs of all the students so that they may understand and help shape their present and future lives. In so doing, we dedicate ourselves to the development of learning programs which provide for child-centered instruction relevant to the needs of middle school students.
>
> The students in our school are involved in a transition from childhood to adolescence. We shall endeavor to help students to better understand and adapt to their ever changing physical needs and to better understand themselves and others regardless of racial, ethnic, and socio-economic differences.
>
> Our students reside in neighborhoods which are undergoing a period of transition and mobility. It is, therefore, our belief that community involvement is necessary to help us create the kind of atmosphere and experience that will contribute to a successful program.

GOALS:
1. To provide the opportunity for students to develop and master those skills basic to full participation in society.
2. To provide the opportunity for students to acquire the basic knowledge necessary to understand their present environment and to prepare themselves for life in future environments.

3. To provide the opportunity for students to learn, develop, and practice those interpersonal skills needed to understand and accept ethnic, racial, and socio-economics groups other than their own.
4. To provide the opportunity for students to learn and utilize independent study skills.
5. To provide an atmosphere conducive to the educational development of the students regardless of racial, ethnic, or socio-economic differences or modes of learning.
6. To recognize that reading, writing, and computing are skills basic to success in our society and that the teaching of them is not restricted to any one academic discipline but is rather a shared responsibility.
7. To provide students with remedial help as needed.
8. To develop a wide range of exploratory activities for socializing, developing interests, and enriching leisure experiences throughout life.
9. To diagnose and evaluate progress of all students in the areas of organized knowledge, basic skills, and personal development.
10. To provide a homebase program and a teacher-advisor to aid students in decision making.
11. To create a learning setting relatively free from the pressures of sophisticated and highly organized social events.
12. To provide an opportunity for individual creativity.
13. To provide an adequate and secure transition between elementary school and high school.
14. To stimulate a career awareness in individual students.
15. To create a flexible organizational program to allow for:
    a. individualized learning
    b. interdisciplinary teams
    c. team teaching
    d. rearrangement of time, space, material, and people.
16. To involve the community in implementing the middle school program.
17. To provide systems of communications for parents and students which will result in a better understanding of the school goals and will enable students to achieve in a positive manner, both academically and in their personal development.

In formulating the philosophy and goals, those responsible should utilize the five facets of the implementation model, namely: (1) reflect the conceptual basis or theory described in the literature, (2) involve leadership from administrative/supervisory personnel, (3) actively involve teachers in the process, (4) make this the basis of the goal-setting process, and (5) make this a basis for future assessment/evaluation.

RATIONALE

A rationale is defined as an explanation or exposition of the principles of some opinion. In the case of middle schools, the rationale should give the reason for choosing the middle school plan and, more importantly, how this plan will be achieved.

A rationale should carefully reflect the total curriculum of a middle school and answer these key questions:
1. Why is the middle school organization desirable?
2. How is a program that meets the needs of the early adolescent learner best designed?

A rationale might include the following sample sub-headings with explanation:

1. *Interdisciplinary teams*—This approach is designed to break down the artificial curriculum barriers and create effective skill reinforcement for the student. This approach provides an effective bridge from the elementary school to high school but also provides for some departmentalization of subject matter.
2. *Grouping*—Grouping patterns are flexible. These are determined by aptitudes, interests and capabilities of students, teacher recommendations, and parent concerns.
3. *Curriculum*—The school attempts to capitalize on the characteristics of the early adolescent learner by encouraging a wide variety of opportunities for learning. Instruction is planned to meet the needs of individual students and is related to immediate goals. The middle school curriculum considers the student's self-concept, self-responsibility, attitudes toward school, and personal happiness.
4. *Flexible scheduling*—Flexible scheduling is an integral part of the middle school organization. Scheduling can be arranged to best suit the needs of students. Time allotments are left to the discretion of teachers.
5. *Independent study*—Independent study is a necessary tool to challenge those students who are ready to extend their intellectual growth in a curriculum area. Since every student may not be ready for this type of program, the final decision for approval should be left to the teacher after consultation with the guidance counselor, parents, and the students involved.
6. *Media services*—These services enable students to become acquainted with appropriate materials for class assignments, projects, or leisure reading. Librarians work closely with the teachers of the interdisciplinary teams, especially to promote literature appreciation and recreational reading.
7. *Home-base advisory program*—The home-base advisory program is utilized to provide a teacher-advisor for each student. The purposes are providing guidance in decision-making, helping students to evaluate their own progress, and fostering interpersonal skills. Middle school students benefit from close identification with an adult.
8. *Guidance services*—The personal development of the adolescent is an extremely important responsibility of the school. The guidance department plays a major role in implementing the learning process, placing students in classes, and providing the necessary testing for the evaluation of the student. Every teacher should be a counselor.

9. *Special interest and club programs*—Middle school students must have the opportunity to develop hobbies and interests as part of the learning program. The club program provides pupils with an opportunity for more depth and exposure in interest areas.

In designing a rationale for the middle school concept, those responsible should utilize the five facets of the implementation model, namely: (1) reflect the conceptual basis or theory described in the literature, (2) involve leadership from administrative/supervisory personnel, (3) actively involve teachers in the process, (4) make this the basis of the goal-setting process, and (5) make this a basis for future assessment evaluation.

SUMMARY

A definition of a middle school, a needs assessment, a statement of philosophy and goals, and a rationale are needed to serve as the foundation for an effective middle school program. In developing these documents, the following general steps are suggested:
1. Define the task.
2. Plan a tentative strategy to achieve the task. Include representation of groups who may be able to make a significant contribution.
3. Follow the strategy design.
4. Present the preliminary findings to the total group.
5. Make the necessary revisions and continue with strategy.
6. Present the revised report to the total group for feedback.
7. Finalize the report and orient the necessary constituency groups.

Chapter VIII
An Effective Middle School...

Possesses A Definite Curriculum Plan That Includes
Factual Information Or Organized Knowledge,
Skills, And Personal Development Activities That
Can Be Correlated With Each Other

Middle school is a curricular issue more than an organizational issue. Middle school means more than sending the ninth grade to the high school, receiving the sixth grade from the elementary school, and changing the name of the school from "junior high" to "middle." Middle school is an approach to the learning process which involves curriculum theory that responds to the learning needs of the early adolescent student.

A long range goal for middle school curriculum is the creation and implementation of an interdisciplinary, thematic approach to learning. Students must be helped to see the wholeness of learning, the interrelationships between subject areas, and the extent to which middle school curriculum addresses the learning needs of the early adolescent learner. The core curriculum approach is an excellent way to respond to student needs and the totality of curriculum. On a daily basis, however, teachers need to work together in team planning periods to correlate content, skills, and personal development topics so that students can see the wholeness that exists in knowledge. The theoretical issues of implementing middle school curriculum should ultimately become the basis for organizational models for the middle school.

Dr. William Alexander provided a model for curriculum for grades 6, 7 and 8 that is both responsive to and consistent with the unique learning needs of the early adolescent. As Dr. Alexander and his colleagues studied the physical, intellectual, social-emotional, and moral needs of middle level students, it was apparent that curriculum must respond to the uniqueness of the early adolescent learner. The model that emerged included three components—organized knowledge, skills, and personal development.

ORGANIZED KNOWLEDGE

Organized knowledge refers to factual information or subject matter. The middle school student is ready for a more intensive focus on learning and retaining factual information. Additionally, students at this level must learn the necessary strategies to secure factual information in future settings. In light of the explosion of knowledge, it is critical that one be prepared to learn information that will be discovered in future years.

Organized knowledge includes the content in all courses in the curriculum—English, social studies, mathematics, science, French, Spanish, art, music, home economics, physical education, technology education or industrial arts, or any other course in the directory. To understand adequately the world around them and to make intelligent decisions, middle school students must have a grasp of organized knowledge.

SKILLS

Middle school teachers have a major responsibility for teaching skills to their students. The teaching of skills does not end with the termination of the elementary grades; in fact, the teaching of skills must be carefully integrated with instruction at the secondary school level and beyond. The teaching of reading is, of course, one of these skills. Reading instruction must include an emphasis on vocabulary development, comprehension, study skills, and functional reading. Additionally, students must be competent in writing, computing, listening, and reference skills. In various classroom situations, the teacher is responsible for developing a readiness for skill development in addition to the readiness for presenting factual information. The middle school needs an organized, systematic effort to teach skills.

PERSONAL DEVELOPMENT

Personal development refers to information and activities needed by the early adolescent to better understand the growth and development taking place at this significant time. The underlying thesis is that the more the early adolescent understands the changes beginning to occur, the better the student will be in coping with or adjusting to these changes.

Each subject area should have topics or units that address the personal development issue for middle school students. For example, a language arts unit entitled "The Outsider" or a unit in French I entitled "Going to School in France" would help the student learn about these developmental problems. Additionally, all of the teachers of the interdisciplinary team or, in some cases, all of the teachers of the school should work together to present the home-base or teacher—advisory program which is a major aspect of this personal development phase of middle school curriculum.

Application #1

There are two applications of Alexander's model. In Application #1, the curriculum for each subject area should include experiences in the categories of organized knowledge, skills, and personal development. In the science curriculum at each grade level, for example, there must be definite examples of organized knowledge, skills, and personal development apparent to the student as well as to the teacher. Curriculum leaders and teachers should examine each subject area to identify how balanced that area is in terms of the three segments. Certain additions or deletions may be needed to balance a subject such as English 7 or Social Studies 8 relative to organized knowledge, skills, and/or personal development. Those who analyze curriculum should also be able to assess the relevancy of the content in each of these three categories to the maturity level of the students.

Application #2

The second application involves the functioning of an interdisciplinary team as it implements or delivers curriculum. A team of teachers should make every effort to correlate organized knowledge, skills, and personal development topics in each of the four or five areas for which they are responsible within the team's structure. Correlation helps pupils see the relationships that exist among the topics, units, or subjects studied. Correlation can and should occur as teachers deliver content, skills, and the home-base program on a day-by-day basis. Ideally, curriculum bulletins should be written on an interdisciplinary basis. If not, teachers should discuss summaries or the highlights of their subject areas in team planning meetings to create a composite picture of the correlations possible.

The following chart is an example of how content in several units in English 7 can be correlated with topics in social studies, science, and mathematics at the same grade level.

ENGLISH GRADE 7

ENGLISH	SOCIAL STUDIES	SCIENCE	MATHEMATICS
1. Stereotypes in Fact and Fiction	Africa	Scientists; Experimenting	Decimals; Graphs
2. Designs in Art and Poetry	Africa		Geometry
3. Knights and Champions	Europe	Building Models	Gathering Data; Measurement
4. Conflict: The Heart of the Matter	Africa; Middle East	Analyzing Data	Probability
5. Communication	Africa; Middle East; Russia	Experimenting	Math Symbols; Word Problems

Another approach to correlating curriculum is provided by Alberty (1962). Alberty listed five types of correlation that could be utilized as an adjunct to Application #2 of Alexander's model.

Type 1 Separate subjects are required of all students in a traditional way, but these subjects are taught by a team of teachers common to a particular group of learners. Example: An English, social studies, mathematics, and science teacher are assigned the same 110 students for four or five periods during the day. These teachers may be provided with team planning time so that content or skills can be correlated.

Type 2 There is a correlation of subjects in such a way that while still teaching their individual subjects all teachers utilize a common theme. The English, social studies, mathematics, and science teachers, in addition to presenting the curriculum for that content area, may also work together to present a unit on "Understanding Myself and Others," "Conservation of Natural Resources," or "Assuming Responsibility in the Family, School, and Community." This approach might also be considered multi-disciplinary.

Type 3 There is a fusion of subjects into units dealing with either cultural or historical themes or major social problems in such a way that teachers approach the unit without regard for their subject specialties and subject matter is drawn from any appropriate source or discipline. In this type, one teacher may be responsible for teaching English and social studies to two or three sections of students while another teacher might be assigned to teach mathematics and science to those same sections. In planning for instruction, the English/social studies teacher may present a unit on "The Colonial Period" or "The Industrial Revolution" by drawing on content from both English and social studies. It is also possible for one teacher to be responsible for the English, social studies, mathematics, and science curriculum for a single class of students. This type is most likely to be found in grades five and six of the middle school.

Type 4 Units are organized around youth needs drawn from real life situations. Again, a teacher responsible for two or more subjects may pull content from those two or more areas to present units such as "Developing Personal Values" or "The Outsider." Type 4 units are an effort to deal directly with the developmental needs, problems, and concerns of early adolescent students.

Type 5 These units are not preplanned but constructed on the basis of student interest and identified through cooperative student-teacher planning.

Application #2 also includes a focus on the skills and personal development programs. Students benefit when a team of teachers works cooperatively to teach and/or reinforce skills. A skill-of-the-week program enables all of the teachers on a team to coordinate their efforts to introduce, reinforce, and evaluate a skill taught in the context of each subject area. Each member of the teaching team utilizes opportunities during that week to teach or reinforce certain aspects of that skill. The student quickly realizes that the skill is important in all subject areas and thus there is purpose for mastering that skill.

Potential skills for such a program are: (1) reading for main ideas, (2) manuscript form, (3) distinguishing between fact and opinion, (4) predicting results, (5) writing a topic sentence, (6) use of the card catalogue in the library, and (7) word capitalization.

Finally, teachers are also encouraged to work together to deliver a personal development program or, as it is most commonly referred to, the home-base or advisor/advisee program. Generally, home-base activities help students adjust to the middle school and/or the interdisciplinary team, understand developmental processes, or resolve certain problems that are typical of the age group. Topics frequently included in such a

program are:
- (1) Decision Making
- (2) Resolving Conflict
- (3) Careers
- (4) Understanding Myself and Others
- (5) Communication Skills
- (6) High School Orientation

CURRICULUM EVALUATION

Interdisciplinary teams, schools, and/or school districts are encouraged to follow the model of the Baltimore County, Maryland Public Schools in conducting an intensive curriculum evaluation. At a time when books about education appear on best seller lists, this school district is involved in a year long study to analyze the curriculum content and methodology as they relate to the educational needs of students. Questions were formulated to determine whether there is too much material to teach, whether the interdisciplinary coordination is as refined as it should be, whether the K-12 sequence is adequately coordinated, and whether more emphasis should be placed on an expanded bank of factual information.

Under the leadership of Superintendent Robert Y. Dubel, the district is embarking upon a vertical as well as a horizontal analysis of curriculum. Vertically, the curriculum of each content area will be carefully analyzed with regard to scope and sequence, factual information, skill development, and other appropriate areas.

Horizontally, the program of each grade level will be reviewed in light of the impact of the curriculum on the learner. Thus, the program of studies for grades 6, 7, and 8 will be carefully analyzed in light of the learning needs and potential of students at those grade levels.

ACTIVITIES

The activities for this chapter provide an opportunity to gain an understanding of the conceptual basis or theory described in the literature. Alexander's model is not only a response to the needs of the early adolescent but, more importantly, serves as a guide for planning middle grades curriculum. The activities at the end of this chapter will enable the reader to learn, practice, and apply the curricular principles.

Administrative/supervisory personnel play a key role in providing leadership for curriculum development, implementation, and/or evaluation. Working under the direction of administrative/supervisory personnel, teachers can be actively involved in the various phases of the curriculum process. The expertise of teachers in knowing the students as well as in delivering the curriculum should become the basis of involving teachers in the activities included at the end of this chapter.

Middle school curriculum cannot be revised or implemented as an instant process. Goals must be set for the various stages of curriculum assessment, design, and implementation. A school or school district must, therefore, have a long range plan for developing a viable middle school curriculum that is fully responsive to the learning needs of early

adolescents. In moving toward these long range goals, these questions must be answered:
(1) Where are we now?
(2) Where would we like to be?
(3) What steps are necessary to reach our goal(s)?

Teachers must be actively involved in all phases of this process. The Baltimore County model could serve as an example for this process.

Activity #1:

This activity is designed to help teachers understand and practice Application #1 of Alexander's model. Teachers should work by departments to complete the chart below. Only major topics or skills should be listed for each subject at each grade level.

Grade _____ Subject _____

Organized Knowledge
1.
2.
3.
4.
5.
6.
7.
8.
9.
10.

Skills
1.
2.
3.
4.
5.
6.
7.
8.
9.
10.

Personal Development
1.
2.
3.
4.
5.
6.
7.
8.
9.
10.

Activity #2:

To help an interdisciplinary group of teachers utilize Application #2 or identify correlations on a regular, systematic basis, the following model is suggested:

ORGANIZED KNOWLEDGE TOPIC _____
  English:
  Mathematics:
  Social Studies:
  Science:

SKILL TOPIC _____
  English:
  Mathematics:
  Social Studies:
  Science:

PERSONAL DEVELOPMENT TOPIC _____
  English:
  Mathematics:
  Social Studies:
  Science:

Using the model above, a common major topic would be selected for organized knowledge, skills, and personal development. Then, each subject area would indicate how that subject area could reinforce the common theme through material drawn from that area.

Activity #3:

Teachers should be provided an opportunity to work in grade level groups to plan for the correlation of content. Following the example of the chart for English 7, teachers should be able to create a correlation chart for all subjects within the curriculum. For each subject area, the various units of study should be listed. As a result, teachers will be able to identify the correlations possible by grade level. As future curriculum is written, these charts may be helpful in moving toward an interdisciplinary or thematic approach.

Activity #4:

To facilitate the skills portion of Alexander's curriculum model, teachers should list all of the skills taught in each subject area. This will facilitate Application #1 of Alexander's model. Then, teachers should identify skills that appear on two or more lists. In this way, teachers are identifying potential skill-of-the-week topics for the interdisciplinary team.

Activity #5:

To facilitate the home-base or teacher/advisory portion of Alexander's curriculum model, teachers should list personal development topics for each subject area. Those topics that appear on two or more lists may be considered for the schoolwide home-base or teacher/advisory program. Certain topics may be more appropriate for one of the grades. Other topics may be so important that they are included in the home-base curriculum for all three grades.

Activity #6:

Interdisciplinary teams, schools, or school districts should conduct a curriculum analysis to ascertain whether the curriculum responds to the learning needs of the early adolescent student. To answer this question, the curriculum analysis should include an examination of each subject area as well as a focus on the total learning program for each grade level. Teachers should assess where the curriculum is in relationship to where the curriculum should be in terms of responding to the needs of students. If a home-base program exists, it should be carefully analyzed to assess the extent to which it responds to the needs of early adolescents. The curriculum analysis project should determine the extent to which the curriculum is balanced by subject and by grade level with regard to the needs of students. This can be accomplished by answering these questions:

(1) What topics can be added by subject area and by grade level?
(2) Is the curriculum balanced in terms of organized knowledge, skills, and personal development?
(3) How will curriculum revision occur?
(4) How will teachers be prepared to implement these changes?
(5) How will the change process be evaluated?

Chapter IX

An Effective Middle School...

**Has A Clearly Established Program Of Studies
Based Upon The Concept Of Exploration
And Provides Opportunities For Student Growth**

As a result of the analysis of early adolescent needs and the theoretical process of implementing a curriculum model, a clearly established program of studies emerges. Program of studies refers to the listing of courses offered for students at a particular grade level. In grade 6, for example, the course format might be:

Grade 6

Subjects	Periods Per Week
Reading and Language Arts	10
Social Studies	5
Mathematics	5
Science	5
Physical Education	5
Art/Music Exploratory	5
	35

Inherent in creating a list such as this one is the rationale for the decisions made. In the above example, the school day consists of 7 periods, science and social studies are offered as full year courses, students have physical education every day, and the exploratory program does not include industrial arts, home economics, and foreign language. Both philosophical and practical considerations are involved in these decisions.

For the middle grades, considerations involved in establishing a program of studies are: (1) the concept of exploration, (2) the role of electives, (3) the utilization of a paradigm for creating the program of studies at each grade level, (4) the provision of opportunities for student growth within specific content areas, and (5) the determination of time during the day for extra-curricular and intramural programs.

THE CONCEPT OF EXPLORATION

Responding to the developmental nature of early adolescents, writers on middle school curriculum advocate emphasis on exploration. Pupils should be encouraged to study a variety of subjects or topics during each year of middle school. In addition, each subject should permit the greatest possible breadth and depth of content within the capacity of the student. As students move from grades 6 through 8, they must have continuous and sequential opportunities to explore various interest areas. This concept should apply to all courses in the curriculum.

Exploratory experiences provide opportunities to satisfy the rapidly changing interests and natural curiosity of this age group, to bring elements of the extra-curricular program to all students during the regular school day, and to enrich learning. The exploratory model originated with the desire to introduce various short term courses during the middle grades, paving the way for more informed decisions on electives at the high school level.

Another key aspect of the exploratory program is the provision of opportunities for students to assess their strengths and weaknesses. Participation in a required complement of experiences enables the student to identify likes and potential areas of expertise. With help, even areas of initial difficulty can become potential strengths.

The concept of exploration is reflected in the approach to a number of courses that need to be scheduled on a parallel basis within the master schedule. Courses such as art, music, industrial arts or technology education, home economics, health, physical education, photography, computers, and foreign language appreciation typically comprise the exploratory program. Pupils should have an opportunity to take all of these courses on an alternate day, quarter, or semester basis at some point during the middle grades.

THE ROLE OF ELECTIVES

For some, electives are seen as the opposite of the concept of exploration. This is not the case. Despite a belief in the concept of required exploratory experiences, many schools also offer students some choices in the course selection process. A student may, for example, choose between French I and Spanish I or between general music and chorus.

Many middle level schools are in the process of moving away from a highly elective program in which students chose three or four of the seven or eight courses in the program of studies for that grade level. In many of these situations, the electives became the major determinant of the entire schedule. For example, because a student elected French I, Wood II, physical education, and chorus, the student may have not been eligible to participate in an interdisciplinary team for English, social studies, mathematics, and science. The issue is the extent to which the scheduling of electives becomes the major force in the total scheduling process for the student, grade level, or entire school.

Pupils should have some choices but in a controlled, systematic fashion. With proper guidance, pupils should be able to make choices for the formal study of a foreign language (French I, Spanish I, Latin I) or music (chorus, general music, orchestra, or band). In some instances, pupils may choose an area of interest in science such as earth science, biology, or physical science. The schedule must be such that students can be placed in a limited number of electives and still receive the proper placement in the required courses.

In moving from an elective to a required exploratory cycle, schools should consider using the wheel approach whereby art, music, industrial arts, and home economics are taken in alternate quarters. Also, a conflict matrix may be used in analyzing the registration data to determine how the pieces of the schedule will fit together to meet the needs of all students within the building.

A PARADIGM FOR CREATING THE PROGRAM OF STUDIES

Schools benefit from the use of a sequential process when making program decisions. A number of issues need to be resolved prior to initiating the five step paradigm suggested. These issues to be resolved are:

(1) The semantic problem with the common learnings or core curriculum approach to English, social studies, mathematics, science, reading, and/or foreign language courses. In addition to determining which courses should be included in the package, a label should be given to this basic portion of the program.

(2) Once a decision is made regarding the name for this curriculum component, consideration should be given to utilizing the block-of-time approach and the extent to which Alexander's model may be used to correlate content, skills, and personal development topics.

(3) A name is also needed for those courses outside of the common learnings package. A name is needed for physical education, art, music, industrial arts, home economics, and other courses so that these teachers feel that they are an integral part of the total middle school organization.

(4) Another issue to be resolved is scheduling the home-base curriculum. Will it be organized as a separate course? How often will it meet? Homebase can be taught by all teachers within the school or just the teachers of the common learnings program. The common learnings teachers can find time within the block-of-time to direct these experiences.

(5) Will reading be taught as a separate course and in which grade levels? Will it be taught through the content areas in one or more grade levels?

(6) Should a definite time be established daily or weekly for a team effort to address skill development?

(7) Prior to finalizing decisions about the program of studies, serious discussion is needed on the topics of team planning and team teaching. These judgments should clearly be reflected in programmatic decisions, especially the periods per week table.

Once these issues are resolved, the following process can be used to create the program of studies. Examples are provided to illustrate potential responses to these key questions. A step-by-step approach is strongly encouraged.

1. What are the elements, components, or courses in the common learnings program for each grade level? How many periods per week will each course be offered?"

SUBJECTS	GRADE 6	GRADE 7	GRADE 8
Language Arts			
Reading			
Social Studies			
Science			
Mathematics			
Foreign Language			
Home-Base			
Skill Development			

2. What courses will be offered in addition to the common learnings? How many periods per week will each course be offered?

SUBJECTS	GRADE 6	GRADE 7	GRADE 8
Art			
Music			
Foreign Language			
Physical Education			
Industrial Arts			
Home Economics			
Computers			
Other _____			

3. Which of the courses outside of common learnings will be required for all students? Which will be elective?

SUBJECTS	GRADE 6	GRADE 7	GRADE 8
Required			

Elective

4. Will there be an activity period within the regular school day? If so, how will it be organized?
5. Does the resulting program of studies meet the requirements of the local and state educational units?

PROVIDING OPPORTUNITIES FOR STUDENT GROWTH WITHIN SPECIFIC CONTENT AREAS

The program of studies provides opportunities for student growth within content areas and by grade level in terms of organized knowledge, skills, and personal development. The selection of units of study for each course at each grade level should be based on the needs of students, the concept of exploration, and the goal of creating well-rounded young adults who can function in society. Units should reflect a thematic approach to the totality of the learning process.

Examples are offered from three subject areas. In physical education, some units are required at a particular grade level (R) while others are elective (E).

SCIENCE

Grade 6:
1. What is Science?
2. Basic Measuring Skills
3. Light and Color
4. Nutrition and the Digestive System
5. Electricity and Magnetism
6. Police/Student Relations
7. Oceanography
8. Family Life

Grade 7:
1. Basic Skills in Science
2. Model of Matter
3. Meteorology
4. Characteristics of Living Things
5. Diversity of Living Things
6. How Things Work
7. Drug and Alcohol Resistance Education (D.A.R.E.)
8. Human Systems

Grade 8:
1. Energy and the Environment
2. Chemistry
3. Geology
4. Ecology of the Chesapeake Bay

PHYSICAL EDUCATION

	Grade 6	Grade 7	Grade 8
Orientation	R	R	R
Team Sports			
Basketball	R	R	E
European Team Handball	R	E	E
Field Hockey		R	E
Flag/Touch Football		R	E
Lacrosse		R	E
Soccer	R	E	E
Softball		R	E
Speedball		R	E
Volleyball	R	R	E
Stick Skills	R		

(Field Hockey, Floor Hockey, STX Lacrosse)

	Grade 6	Grade 7	Grade 8
Individual Sports			
Archery			R
Aquatics	R	R	R
Badminton	R	E	E
Bowling	E	E	E
Leisure Running		R	E

	Grade 6	Grade 7	Grade 8
Gymnastics	R	R	E
Recreational Games	R		
Stunts and Tumbling	R		
Table Tennis		E	E
Tennis		R	R
Track and Field		R	R
Tumbling and Pyramids		R	E
Wrestling		R	R
Rhymthic Activities			
Basic Movements	R	E	E
Aerobic Dance		R	E
Contemporary Dance		R	
Folk Dancing			R
Modern Dance			R
Square Dance		R	E
Aerobic Fitness			
Body Conditioning	R	E	E
Weight Training		R	E
First Aid	R		
Adaptive Physical Education			
Modified Physical Education, Exercise, and Weight Control	R	R	R
Fitness Training	R	R	R
Outdoor Experiences			
Angling	E	E	E
Backpacking	E	E	E
Campcrafts	E	E	E
Canoeing	E	E	E
Hiking	E	E	E
Orienteering	E	E	E
Cycling	E	E	E

ART

In this model for art education, there are six major content areas that are continuous in grades 6, 7, and 8. The areas involve sequential experiences in drawing, painting, printmaking, lettering, crafts, and sculpture. Notice the sequential development of the major curriculum thrust.

1. Drawing
    Grade 6—Demonstrate an understanding of ways drawing techniques may be used to represent the characteristics of real or imagined forms
    Grade 7—Demonstrate an understanding of composition in drawing.
    Grade 8—Demonstrate an understanding of ways to achieve specific effects in drawing.

2. Painting
    Grade 6—Demonstrate an understanding of ways artists consider color properties and use painting techniques.
    Grade 7—Demonstrate an understanding of composition in painting.
    Grade 8—Demonstrate an understanding of ways that specific effects may be created through the use of techniques and materials in painting.

3. Printmaking
    Grade 6—Demonstrate an understanding of techniques used to create a print.
    Grade 7—Demonstrate an understanding of ways that design principles may be applied in creating a print.
    Grade 8—Demonstrate an understanding of ways that materials, processes, and design principles are used to achieve specific effects in printmaking.

4. Lettering
    Grade 6—Demonstrate an understanding of lettering styles and techniques.
    Grade 7—Demonstrate an understanding of ways that design principles may be applied to lettering.
    Grade 8—Demonstrate an understanding of factors that influence the selection and design of letters in the solution of an art problem.

5. Sculpture
    Grade 6—Demonstrate an understanding of basic techniques of materials used in designing sculptural forms.
    Grade 7—Demonstrate an understanding of ways forms are arranged and treated in sculpture.
    Grade 8—Demonstrate an understanding of factors that influence the selection and use of materials and techniques to create sculptural forms.

6. Crafts
    Grade 6—Demonstrate an understanding of basic processes and techniques used in designing craft objects.
    Grade 7—Demonstrate an understanding of ways design principles may be applied in creating a craft object.
    Grade 8—Demonstrate an understanding of the factors that influence the selection of processes and techniques to create craft objects.

EXTRACURRICULAR ACTIVITIES/INTRAMURALS

To complete the program of studies issue from both the theoretical and practical viewpoints, decisions are needed relative to the extracurricular/intramurals program. Participation in student government, an intramural basketball game, the French club, a computer club, and a quiz bowl team are important aspects of a student's experience at the middle level.

To fulfill the personal development phase of middle school curriculum, schools need to include clubs, special interest activities, and an intramural program. The real issue is whether these activities should be scheduled during the regular school day, before school, or after school. In many districts, time is provided during the regular day for these experiences because students are transported or because of a genuine commitment to including all students in this phase of the curriculum. In other situations, the program is organized on a before or after school basis.

The intramural program offers an opportunity for all students to extend skills acquired in physical education. For example, upon completion of the basketball unit, students may participate in a tournament based upon their skill development level. Teams could be formed within physical education classes, homerooms, interdisciplinary teams, or on a random basis to enable students to compete under the careful supervision of those physical education teachers who recently taught the unit. An extensive intramural program gives students opportunities to extend skills in all phases of physical education and interact with peers in a structured situation.

ACTIVITIES

In making decisions about the program of studies, educators should consider the five facets of the implementation model. An understanding of exploration, the role of electives, the paradigm for creating the program of studies, providing opportunities for student growth in specific content areas, and extra-curricular activities/intramurals is needed in completing each of these activities. Administrative/supervisory personnel should provide the necessary leadership, and there should be ample opportunities for faculty participation. In moving from the status quo to a desired model for the future, goal-setting is vital to insure a step-by-step approach that has the support of all constituency groups. Finally, assessment and evaluation should be conducted throughout each of these activities to render data that may be needed at a future time.

Activity #1:
Develop a definition of the concept of exploration and describe how the concept of exploration will be implemented in the school or district. This can become part of the rationale.

Activity #2:
Following the paradigm, develop a program of studies for each grade. Write a brief rationale for the decisions made.

Activity #3:
After the program of studies has been developed, design a public relations program to inform parents and citizens of the community about the decisions made. In the presentation, demonstrate how this program of studies is connected to the elementary as well as the high school experiences.

Activity #4:
Once the program of studies has been developed, list the potential units

of study by subject and grade level to reflect growth, maturation, and developmental needs of students in grades 6, 7, and 8. Include a rationale to indicate how the concept of exploration is reflected in the program of studies.

Activity #5:
Write a series of recommendations reflecting the program of studies for those individuals responsible for creating the master schedule. In these recommendations, suggest teaming options to be utilized, priorities for block-of-time scheduling, the rationale for a 6, 7, 8 or 9 period day, and the need for modular subdivisions of time.

Activity #6:
Write a position paper on the home-base program. State the organizational plan for this program, responsibilities of teachers and administrators, how curriculum will be developed, and how the program will be evaluated. This position paper may also be included in the rationale and/or philosophy statement.

Activity #7:
Design a master plan for the extra-curricular and intramural programs for the school. Determine whether this program will be before, during, or after the school day. Include a listing of all the activities, a blueprint for motivating student participation, a provision for students to participate in more than one activity during the course of the school year, and a procedure to evaluate the programs.

Chapter X

An Effective Middle School . . .

**Builds On The Strengths Of Elementary Education And
Prepares Students For Success In High School**

A transitional phase, the middle school is the link between the elementary and high schools. Elementary students experience six years, including kindergarten, in the same building. During that time, they have become acquainted with the learning process and, for the most part, have learned to feel very secure in that setting. The physical move from elementary to middle school occurs at a time when many students are undergoing major developmental transformations.

In the eyes of many, middle level education is to prepare students for high school where a highly departmentalized learning situation prepares students for college or the world of work. In high school, students are expected to be successful in both the curricular and extra-curricular phases of school life. With the onset of adolescence, these young people are expected to be both independent and mature in their approach to responsibilities.

The middle school must be viewed as a distinct entity. Students must be adequately prepared for the transition to and from the middle level. Educators must focus on both articulation and orientation as methods of achieving this aspect of an effective middle school. The goal is for students to move from elementary to middle to high school in the smoothest fashion possible. Articulation focuses on the totality of the learning process and the consistency within a vertical approach to curriculum on a K-12 basis. Curriculum for grades 6, 7, and 8 should be an extension of the elementary program and the prerequisite for high school. Orientation entails preparing the students and their parents for change with a special focus on the psychological readiness of the children to learn and of the parents to support that learning process.

ARTICULATION

Within a school district, educators must focus on the articulation of the curriculum as a K-12 experience. There must be a clear vision, for example, of the mathematics, reading, social studies, and art programs of study in a vertical sense. There must be obvious continuity in terms of content, skill development, and personal development.

In helping students succeed in the middle grades, educational leaders must answer a number of key questions:
  (1) How does the middle school segment fit in with the K-12 curriculum for that district?
  (2) In what ways does the middle school segment serve as an extension of the elementary learning experience?

(3) How does the totality of the middle school curriculum (from the horizontal perspective) meet the unique needs of the early adolescent student?

(4) How does the middle school learning experience prepare students for high school?

The answers should be a continuing subject of discussion. Articulation is most effective when the approach to curriculum development, implementation, and evaluation by the district includes an analysis of the needs of middle school students. Articulation conferences should take place between elementary and middle school personnel and then middle and high school personnel. Throughout these discussions, there should be a focus on the needs of individual students as well as the group as a whole. Follow-up studies are helpful so that teachers will know the successes and weaknesses of their former pupils, and those responsible for supervising the curriculum development process will be able to analyze data for future curriculum changes.

ORIENTATION

Orientation is the preparation for change. This is an important issue because of the anxiety level of students and parents. They fear the unknown. They are leaving a safe, protected environment and need to learn that the environment of the middle school, while different, is equally safe and protected.

Middle school educators should use the following checklist as they examine their orientation program to identify the factual information that students and parents should know to prepare for the new environment.

1. General description of the building
2. Location of the sixth grade interdisciplinary teams
3. Locations of the other classrooms where sixth graders will have the exploratory program
4. Expectations of teachers
5. What middle school students are like
6. Program of studies for sixth graders
7. Orientation program for incoming sixth graders
8. Social life of the school
9. Extracurricular and intramural programs
10. Discipline policy
11. Attendance policy
12. Grading policy
13. Transportation arrangements

Beginning with the winter of the fifth grade year and extending through the first month of the sixth grade, these ideas are proposed as examples of orientation activities:

- **Orient elementary school administrators and fifth grade teachers about the middle school program**

  These individuals play a major role in preparing students and parents for the middle school. They know the students well; and more importantly, students and parents have confidence in the counsel of these individuals. Time invested in orienting elementary school personnel about the middle school program will pay major dividends during the transition

- **Gather data for needs assessment**
  This activity is part of the articulation as well as the orientation processes. In designing the instructional program for an incoming group of students, it is essential to review data which can be compiled jointly by elementary and middle school personnel. Unique needs of groups of students as well as individuals should be identified.

- **Fifth grade students visit the middle school in the spring of the year, visit classes, and participate in a typical day**
  Generally held in the spring of the year, these activities provide incoming sixth graders the chance to visit the middle school, meet some of the teachers, learn about the program, and become familiar with expectations. This will help to reduce some of the fear of the unknown.

- **Presentations at elementary schools by students, counselors, and administrators of middle schools**
  This activity can precede the visit to the middle school, can be a substitute for a visit to the middle school, or can be a follow-up to that visit. Middle school students, preferably those who previously attended that elementary school, can describe their experiences as sixth graders. They can also be "experts" in answering questions of fifth graders.

- **Parent meeting in winter or spring**
  Once the registration process begins, parents are anxious to learn about the middle school program. A meeting in January or February is not too early to begin to make parents aware of the sixth grade program and the expectations of the middle school. As parents begin to gain more information, their anxiety level will diminish and they can begin to help their children prepare for entry to the middle school.

- **Parents visit middle school to see sixth grade classes**
  Either during American Education Week or at designated times, parents of fifth graders could visit sixth grade classes at the middle school. They would be able to observe first hand the methods of teaching and curriculum used in grade 6. Sixth grade teachers could be available at a designated time to answer questions.

- **Individual and group visits during the summer**
  At designated times, teachers could be available during the summer to take students on tours of the building and begin the home-base/advisory program. This provides the opportunity for students to meet others in their homeroom.

- **Open house prior to first day of classes**
  As the start of school approaches, the anxiety level of incoming sixth graders and their parents increases. Thus, either during the day or in the evening, students and parents will welcome the opportunity to visit the middle school. In this visit they will meet such key persons as the principal, assistant principal(s), guidance counselor, nurse, and all of the teachers. Many questions about the first day of school can be answered at this time.

- **Special orientation activities on the first day of school**
  In many middle schools, the first day of school is devoted to orientation activities. Conducted by the homeroom or interdisciplinary team teachers, students have a tour of the school. Students also have an opportunity to receive a brief orientation to each of the courses in the program of studies. Expectations of teachers as well as of the school can be discussed at this time. Students' questions can be answered in a more personalized fashion.

- **Continuing orientation activities conducted by homeroom teachers for the first weeks of school**
  Beyond the first day of school, orientation activities should continue. Students should learn about the library/media center, the role of the nurse, the guidance counselor, and other special services available. The identity of the team can be established and reinforced at this time. By this point, the advisory program should be functioning.

Just as middle school personnel play a key role in the orientation of incoming sixth graders, they also need to assist with the transition of eighth graders to the high school. Eighth grade students are anxious about making a change; and, high school personnel may need assistance in learning how to meet the needs of ninth grade students. In preparation for the transition to ninth grade, pupils need to know about individualized schedules, departmental organization, the extra-curricular program, the social life on campus, course selection procedures, and various grouping arrangements.

Orientation to the high school should include a spring or summer meeting at the high school; assemblies at the middle school featuring high school students, teachers, and counselors; visits to the high school by middle school students; parent information meetings; visits for parents at the high school during the regular school day; a buddy system pairing a new student with an upper classman; and articulation meetings involving middle and high school staff members.

SUMMARY

In order to help students make the necessary transition from the elementary school to the middle school as well as from the middle school to the high school, middle school personnel must assume a leadership role in the articulation and orientation processes. Through articulation, teachers are able to identify how the program for grades 6, 7, and 8 fits in with the K-12 curriculum and meets the unique needs of this age group. Orientation activities are essential as students move into the middle school and then into the high school. Orientation activities must recognize the anxiety level of the students and provide the needed counseling and information to overcome these apprehensions. Via articulation and orientation, the effective middle school builds on the strength of elementary education and prepares students for success in high school.

Activity #1:
A committee of teachers, administrators, counselors, and central office personnel should be formed to write a position paper on the importance of

articulation. This statement should be included in the rationale as well as philosophy statements.

Activity #2:
On-going study committees should be formed to study the articulation process for various aspects of the curriculum. As an outcome, these committees should create guidelines for the on-going study of articulation in each of these areas.

Activity #3:
Design a comprehensive orientation program for incoming sixth graders and their parents. Personnel from the elementary as well as the middle school should be involved. For each activity, there should be a statement of purpose and a method of evaluating the activity.

Activity #4:
Design a comprehensive orientation program for eighth graders as they prepare for high school. Separate activities should also be developed for parents of this group. For each activity, there should be a statement of purpose and a method of evaluating the activity.

Activity #5:
Develop an orientation package for students who transfer into the middle school during the seventh and eighth grades. Activities should be designed to acclimate these students to all aspects of the middle school experience.

Activity #6:
Design a follow-up study of the orientation into the middle as well as into the high school. Data should be gathered from students who have completed the adjustment. These data then can be analyzed to modify the existing orientation programs.

Chapter XI

An Effective Middle School . . .

Employs Teachers Who Focus On The Learning Needs Of Pupils By Using Appropriate Teaching Strategies

Middle school teachers should know the special learning needs of each pupil and utilize appropriate teaching strategies. These approaches should be based upon current research on the developmental patterns of students. During early adolescence, pupils have a short attention span and a low tolerance for fatigue.

Cognitively, pupils are at various stages of development. Many, if not most, are still dependent upon concrete examples and have difficulty with higher levels of abstraction. As a result, teachers must gear their lessons to move from the concrete to the abstract. There should also be a focus on skill development throughout the teaching process.

Teachers must also be aware of the implications of the social-emotional phase. The self-concept of the student is extremely important throughout all dimensions of the program. Group membership is extremely important, and students will go to almost any length to receive the approval of their peers. Independent study opportunities should be available for those students who are ready for advanced supplemental work as well as those who need remedial assistance.

Alexander's curriculum model suggests a number of appropriate teaching strategies. Working in teams, teachers should correlate content so pupils can see the wholeness of learning. In addition to teaching skills in each content area, a skill-of-the-week program should be organized. Teachers play a major role in providing a home-base or teacher/advisory program and should identify opportunities to correlate that phase of the program with their specific content area.

Learning is an active process. Students remember what they did more so than what they heard or read. Finally, relevant strategies should be geared to the individuality of the student and the unique learning style of that individual.

The remainder of this chapter will be divided into three parts—appropriate teaching strategies that should be used by all teachers, strategies that may be utilized under certain conditions in every subject, and thoughts about the learning environment.

AN APPROACH TO DAILY LESSON PLANNING

The following strategies, applicable to all areas, are suggested to address the unique learning needs of early adolescents.
1. *Subdivide the entire period (40-50 minutes) into four or five segments of ten to fifteen minutes each.* For example, mathematics teachers provide a drill for students upon their arrival, check the

drill and homework, introduce new work on a topic, enable pupils to inductively write a rule, provide students the chance to do independent classwork to practice the skill, summarize, and present a homework assignment.

2. *Provide clear, concise structure for all activities.* Pupils must know exactly what to do for each specific activity. In addition to oral directions, teachers should write them on the chalkboard. Teachers should anticipate kinds of questions students will ask, and instructions should be given on a step-by-step basis.

3. *Provide variety within the period.* During the forty or fifty minutes of the lesson, students should not be doing one continuous learning task. Variety is needed to sustain the interest and enthusiasm of the students. This need for variety is closely related to the attention span limitations of students.

4. *Clarify purposes for each activity.* Pupils must know exactly why they are being asked to complete an activity. Once they know the reasons, they are more willing to participate in the activities and assess their performance in relationship to these goals. Without a stated purpose, students may not show the necessary enthusiasm for completing an activity.

5. *Provide adequate motivation, readiness, and goal-setting.* Once purposes are stated, teachers must make an overt effort to initiate the interest and readiness of the students. Lessons should start with a concrete motivational activity. Additionally, it is important for the teacher to monitor students' responses to the motivational activity which should be closely related to the purposes of the lesson. Readiness includes preparation for both the content and skill highlighted. Motivation and readiness are part of a larger concept entitled goal-setting. Both long and short range goals should exist for all instruction.

6. *Utilize recall strategies.* Recall strategies help students connect new material with material already learned. The current lesson should begin with several open-ended questions that review the previous day's lesson. Recall helps students see the connection between prior learning and the goals of the current lesson.

7. *Provide transitions to connect the various activities within the lesson.* An effective lesson consists of several activities designed to accomplish a specific goal or goals. Although the teacher may easily see the relationship, it is essential that students be able to identify this relationship. Thus, transitions should be used to make connections evident to students. A transition usually consists of a summary statement of the previous activity, a preview of the next activity, and a statement of the relationship between the two parts. Transitions should be inductive whenever possible.

8. *Be flexible within structure.* Middle school teachers need to be highly organized. Within the structure, however, teachers must be flexible. There will be times when deviation from the plan is needed.

9. *Know the cognitive level of the students in each classroom.* Teachers should be aware of the cognitive level of each student. Students may be at the pre-operational, concrete onset, concrete mature,

formal onset, and formal mature levels. Teachers should call upon students at appropriate times while helping them to expand their cognitive levels.
10. *Move from the concrete to the abstract in the concept development process.* Concrete examples should be offered at the beginning of lessons or activities within the lesson. Lessons should move from the concrete or specific to the abstract or more theoretical. Pictures, models, advertisements, or slides are concrete. Pupils should be able to see, feel, or touch such examples. As the lesson or activity continues, key questions should be utilized in moving from the concrete to the abstract.
11. *Construct effective questions to accomplish the objectives of the lesson.* In planning for instruction, teachers should create key questions and list them in the lesson plan. Questions should be open-ended and cause pupils to think prior to responding.
12. *Use wait-time effectively.* Wait-time is the length of the silent period after the teacher asks the question and prior to the initial student response. Surprisingly, the average teacher waits only one second for an answer. A longer wait-time would give students an opportunity to formulate an answer; thus, there is a greater chance that more students will participate in the ensuing discussion.
13. *Teach reading skills as part of an organized, systematic process.* All middle school teachers are or should be teachers of reading. Every teacher should teach vocabulary and comprehension skills in the context of the subject. Study skills, functional reading activities, and oral reading opportunities achieve further growth in this important area of skill development. Teachers should be consistent in teaching a directed reading lesson by including the following elements: (1) motivation/readiness for the content as well as the skill, (2) vocabulary development, (3) specific purposes for silent reading, (4) silent reading, (5) discussion of purpose questions, and (6) follow-up activities.
14. *Provide a summary or assessment.* At the end of each activity as well as the end of each lesson, there should be a summary and/or assessment. This can be achieved via a specific activity or a series of directed questions.

STRATEGIES FOR CERTAIN CONDITIONS

In this segment, the additional strategies presented may only be applicable in certain situations.
1. *Student-to-student interaction.* In many secondary classrooms, teaching is characterized by a regular pattern. Typically, the teacher asks a question, a student answers the question, and then the teacher asks an additional question. The middle school classroom should feature many opportunities for student-to-student interaction. Students should interact with one another while solving mathematics problems, completing science laboratory experiments, creating a chart in social studies, or discussing the plot of a novel in English. Physical movement is encouraged to reduce the characteristic restlessness.

2. *Team tasks.* Team or small group experiences are an extension of student-to-student interaction and usually involve groups of students working on specific academic tasks. This approach is a response to the social-emotional development of the age group and can be highly motivational for students who need positive peer pressure to perform.
3. *Team approach to skill development.* Interdisciplinary team teachers should develop a skill-of-the-week approach to skill development. Students benefit from the motivation of the team approach and the reinforcement it provides.
4. *Simulation and game techniques.* Social studies teachers have many opportunities to create simulations. Industrial arts teachers also utilize simulations of the assembly line process to teach both content and skills. Other areas can utilize simulations as well. After a simulation or game experience, the teacher asks numerous questions to help students comprehend and analyze that which occurred.
5. *Use of the inductive method.* In deductive teaching, the teacher explains a rule or principle to the students. Inductive teaching, on the other hand, allows the students to discover the rule by examining data and answering a number of key questions presented by the teacher. Information learned inductively is retained longer than material presented deductively.
6. *Independent study.* Independent study allows students to move at their own pace, explore areas of interest, or work with a group of peers on a project of mutual curiosity. In cooperation with the librarian, any teacher may create an independent study experience for an individual, small group of students, or the entire class.
7. *Peer teaching/peer counseling.* Students may conduct certain parts of the lesson, prepare materials for instruction, or play a major role in a counseling activity. Peer teaching and peer counseling are constructive responses to social-emotional needs.
8. *Enrichment for formal thinkers.* Students who are capable of handling higher levels of abstraction need the additional challenge. Teachers can attain this goal by reserving certain questions for these students, encouraging them to complete independent study projects, assigning supplemental work, and permitting these students to assist the teacher whenever possible.

NATURE OF THE LEARNING ENVIRONMENT

This final section on appropriate teaching strategies includes suggestions for improving the nature of the learning environment based upon the needs of students.
1. *Decorate classrooms appropriate to the subject(s) being taught and the age(s) of the students.* Bulletin boards should reflect topics of study, and student work should be on display. Mobiles and plants add to the environment of the classroom. The goal is to provide an inviting environment for learning.
2. *Utilize flexible scheduling techniques.* Members of the interdisciplinary as well as the exploratory teams should identify opportunities

for flexible scheduling and utilize these whenever possible. All lessons do not have to be for fifty minutes, and special activities can be scheduled to complement the curriculum.
3. *Anticipate and prevent problems.* In planning for instruction, teachers should anticipate potential problems and then work to prevent them.
4. *Encourage risk taking.* Middle school students grow when they have the opportunity to take risks in a secure, protected environment. A caring teacher encourages students to take risks.
5. *Focus on affective issues.* In addition to presenting content material, middle school teachers should also address affective or emotional topics that come up in the course of the learning process. A discussion of a novel in English may prompt a student to share some personal experience.
6. *Inject humor whenever possible.* Teachers should find opportunities to inject humor into the lesson. Humor should always be in good taste and never at the expense of a student or another faculty member.
7. *Praise, don't criticize.* Middle school students respond to praise. Teachers should use varied methods to dispense praise so as not to make the words seem too mechanical. Parents should be informed of the accomplishments of their children. Praise reinforces and facilitates learning.

ACTIVITIES

1. Develop a way to survey the extent to which these techniques are now used in the school or district. Analyze data by department, teaching team, and/or grade level
2. As teachers establish personal teaching goals, they should be encouraged to select strategies from this menu. Teachers should utilize mentoring and peer coaching plans to help them achieve their individual goals. The evaluation process should include opportunities for teachers to enumerate efforts in mastering these strategies.
3. Involve teachers in the identification of additional strategies that respond to the uniqueness of early adolescents and that may be added to the list contained in this chapter.
4. Invite teachers and other staff members at the school and district levels to design research projects on teaching strategies. One of the functions of the district research specialist should be to study this topic. Teachers involved in graduate courses should be encouraged to conduct research on appropriate teaching strategies.

Chapter XII
An Effective Middle School . . .

Creates Teaching Teams Using Block-Of-Time To Best Deliver The Instructional Program

A middle school can be responsive to the needs of students by utilizing some form of team planning/teaching as the school organizes to deliver instruction. A team approach at this level makes it possible to:
- help pupils make the transition from a self-contained elementary classroom to the departmentalization of the secondary grades
- help students see the wholeness that exists in learning, both in content and in skills
- emphasize the child as well as subject matter
- provide consistency to an age group that desperately needs structure and consistency
- create a family-like atmosphere in an age when fewer and fewer students know the real meaning of the word *family*
- facilitate various grouping arrangements for students
- enable teachers to subdivide blocks-of-time to best meet the unique needs of students
- provide for increased professional growth of teachers through cooperative planning, sharing of materials, and cooperative teaching
- provide more opportunities for resource personnel to be directly involved in the instructional program
- provide for the unique guidance needs of early adolescent students

Team teaching involves a group of teachers providing instruction to a common group of students. In some cases, teachers may plan together during common team planning periods but return to their individual classrooms and work independently with their classes. In other cases, teachers can plan and teach cooperatively. Teaming may involve a cluster of teachers working together to correlate content and skills on a regular basis or presenting a thematic unit as they teach different subjects to a common group of students.

TYPES OF TEAMS

There are three types of teams—interdisciplinary, disciplinary or single subject, and core/combination subject teams. In the interdisciplinary approach, two or more teachers work together to coordinate instruction in as many as five subject areas. For example, an English, social studies, mathematics, and science teacher could work together with four teaching sections for a maximum of five periods per day to create an interdisciplinary approach to the content material in those four subject areas.

Benefits of the interdisciplinary approach include:
(1) Students have subject matter specialists for each subject area, but

there is coordination of the total instructional program.
(2) Beyond the standard curriculum guides, thematic interdisciplinary units as well as specific interdisciplinary activities can be planned to meet the needs of pupils.
(3) Teachers can work as a team to focus on the needs of pupils.
(4) Content, skills, and personal development activities can be correlated.
(5) Planning periods can be used for pupil and parent conferences.
(6) A discipline code for the entire team can be consistently implemented.
(7) Block-of-time and flexible scheduling can facilitate fundamental aspects of the program.
(8) Teaching sections can be organized on a homogeneous, heterogeneous, or contiguous basis; regrouping is possible.

A disciplinary or single subject team involves two or more teachers of the same subject area who work together to present that course to two or more sections scheduled at the same time each day. Two Algebra I teachers could, for example, combine their efforts to teach fifty students. Over the course of the year, these students could be regrouped between these two teachers according to the students' strengths and weaknesses that become apparent as the course evolves.

Features of the disciplinary or single subject team are:
(1) Teachers meet on a regular basis to plan and evaluate the instructional program.
(2) Special programs can be developed for the unique needs of pupils in a particular subject area.
(3) Teachers have an opportunity to specialize within that subject area.
(4) Teachers can teach more than one grade level.
(5) Student has more than one teacher for a particular subject.
(6) Opportunities exist for curriculum development and implementation at the local school level.
(7) Experienced teachers can help novices.
(8) Enrichment and remediation can be offered.

A third type is the core/combination subject team. This approach involves two or three teachers for two or three subjects. Examples of core/combination subject teams are: English/social studies or English/social studies/art or art/music. This plan affords more opportunities for large and small group instruction, regrouping within and between subjects, correlation, and the opportunity for a student to spend more time in one of these subject areas.

Activities:
1. For inclusion in the rationale and philosophy statements as well as a working guideline, a group of professionals should define the terms *team teaching, team planning,* and *team organization.*
2. Of the ten reasons for a team organization, which are the most appropriate for this school or school district?
3. In light of the curriculum for the school and/or school district, how will the terms *interdisciplinary, disciplinary, or core/curriculum* be

defined? Which subjects will be taught as an interdisciplinary, disciplinary, or core/curriculum team? What recommendations are there for creating the master schedule?

4. In light of the curriculum for the school and/or district, what are the advantages and limitations of each of the three models of team organization?

BLOCK-OF-TIME

To facilitate any of the types of team organization, block-of-time scheduling should be utilized. Block-of-time permits teachers to teach their classes and be available for planning sessions at the same time.

Some advantages of block-of-time scheduling are:
  (1) each teacher can teach his/her curriculum area
  (2) teachers can correlate content, skills, or personal development activities more easily
  (3) time modules can be adjusted by the decision of the teachers of the team
  (4) pupils can have more time in a certain subject if the situation dictates
  (5) time modules can be adjusted to the needs of the pupils
  (6) films, guest speakers, and assemblies for large groups can be scheduled; yet, each pupil can still see each teacher of the team on that day if the teachers so desire
  (7) there is no problem with missed classes if all pupils on a team are going on a field trip or even if one or two classes go on a field trip
  (8) standardized testing can be scheduled with minimum disruption
  (9) station teaching can be developed for one or more courses without disruption to the other areas
  (10) rotating schedules can be developed for the various sections of the team
  (11) provision can be made for independent study programs
  (12) two or more subjects can be fused together as a core curriculum; subjects can be interrelated with broad themes or skills approaches.

There is a difference between interdisciplinary team organization and block-of-time scheduling. To be an interdisciplinary team, the four or five teachers do not *have* to be scheduled for classes at the same time. Although it is advisable, it is not mandatory. Block-of-time requires that the teachers involved are, in fact, teaching at the same time. Ideally, all interdisciplinary teams (as well as core/combination and disciplinary teams) will be scheduled on a block-of-time basis.

This block-of-time concept must be reflected in the construction of the master schedule, the vehicle to implement the various aspects of the effective middle school. The following steps are suggested in constructing a block-of-time master schedule:

1. Determine the program of studies for each grade level.
2. Make the necessary decisions on team teaching arrangements.
3. Create a preliminary registration form.
4. Determine the grouping procedures.
5. Register the students.
6. Analyze the student request tally sheet.
7. Study the conflict charts.
8. Decide the composition of teams.
9. Write the table of teachers' assignments.
10. Develop a tentative schedule by placing courses on daily/weekly schedules by teams.
11. Assign pupils to teams.
12. Analyze the loading process/assignment of pupils to teams.
13. Make needed adjustments to original schedule.
14. Request additional computer run(s) of the master schedule.
15. Assign homeroom sections within teams and/or grade level.
16. Publish the necessary lists.
17. Orient teachers and students to the master schedule.

Activities:
1. What opportunities will exist for block-of-time instruction? How will these decisions be made? What training will be provided for teachers involved in block-of-time approaches? Using the listing of advantages of the block-of-time approach, several examples should be listed for each of these factors.
2. Who will be involved in constructing the master schedule? What guidelines does the school district provide for scheduling and what local options exist? What is the time chronology for building the schedule?
3. Design a process to evaluate the effectiveness of block-of-time programs as well as the effectiveness of the master schedule.

HELPING TEACHERS WORK AS MEMBERS OF A TEAM

In many cases, the success of a middle school program is related to the effectiveness of the various teaching teams in the school. Many, if not most, middle school teachers have not received training at the undergraduate or graduate levels on the skills needed to function as a member of a team. Yet, teachers must work harmoniously to deliver the instructional program effectively.

This chapter will address a number of skills, activities, and techniques that will help teachers work as members of a team. Topics will include: (1) forming teams, (2) team building, (3) use of planning periods, (4) using the schedule effectively, and (5) sharing the leadership responsibility.

Forming Teams. Teams can be appointed by the principal, or teachers can have an active involvement in the formation of teams. Teacher input in the process frequently suggests a greater feeling of investment on their part. This implies more willingness to work for the success of the team.

Once a decision about team leaders is made, the teachers involved can be assembled and given a chance to form teams. For example, in selecting staff for three interdisciplinary teams in grade 7, three English, three social studies, three science, and three mathematics teachers could be assembled. They could be informed that they are to organize themselves into three teams using three simple criteria—each team must have the best possible race, sex, and experience balance.

In this example, the teachers would meet, formulate the teams, and submit the results to the principal for confirmation. At the end of the school year, teachers could have the opportunity to go through this process again or begin another year with the existing teams.

Activities:
1. Develop a set of guidelines for the formation of teams.
2. Develop a set of guidelines for the selection of team leaders.
3. What is the provision for a teacher to express the wish to serve on a different team?
4. How will the formation of interdisciplinary teams differ from the formation of exploratory teams?

Team Building. Designed to enhance team effectiveness, team building is a process by which persons learn to work effectively to (1) build and maintain a spirit of trust, (2) set and achieve shared goals, and (3) work simultaneously on tasks necessary to the accomplishment of the goals and ultimate maintenance of a trustful climate.

Openness and sharing within the team are critical if trust is to be built. Hidden agendas, poor relationships, and unshared feelings about a task can block team building. Team members must learn to speak openly about their feelings on certain issues.

Six types of team building activities are suggested. These activities should occur early in the process of forming teams and can be repeated as necessary over the life of that team.

Getting to know each other. Team members must really get to know each other despite the fact that they may have known each other previously. To accomplish this goal, team members should talk about their hobbies and interests, families, and feelings about being a member of the team.

Expectations of other team members. In the process of getting to know one another, expectations should be shared. Some team members may be looking for an opportunity to discuss teaching methods while others are seeking support in handling discipline problems.

Expectations of the team leader. Although there are differences in how the team leader is appointed, it is critical for team members to talk about their expectations of the individual who is conducting team meetings. Guidelines should be developed for when there is a deadlock on a particular issue and whether or not the team leader should delegate tasks to members of the team.

Expectations of resource personnel. Guidance counselors, administrators, librarians, reading teachers, and speech/language pathologists are an integral part of the interdisciplinary teaching process. Team members need to explore their expectations of these resource personnel; and, conversely, resource personnel need to explore their expectations of team members.

Procedures to establish team goals. Team building activities also include the opportunity to establish team goals. This level of goal-setting enables the team to respond to the particular needs of the students on that team. Teachers need an opportunity to explore the procedure in establishing these goals.

Consensus needed for team decisions. A final aspect of team building is determining consensus needed for specific decisions. In areas where the team has autonomy, it is essential to designate which issues may require a vote, a simple majority, and which mandate unanimous consent. There may also be times when any teacher on the team may exercise a veto.

Activity:
For each category of team building, an activity or set of activities should be developed to guide teachers through that phase of the process. In addition to designing activities for the outset of the school year, a procedure is needed to determine when supplementary team building activities may be needed during the course of the school year. There is also the need to evaluate these team building activities and the extent to which the goals of these activities are being achieved.

Use of Planning Periods. To be successful, teachers should have a minimum of two or three planning periods per week to accomplish the goals of the team. Teachers should not be asked to cover classes, supervise the cafeteria, or complete written reports during these periods.

Planning periods enhance the instructional program. Teachers may discover ways to correlate topics or units within the various subjects; plan, implement, and evaluate a skills or personal development program; share resources of team members; encourage team members to express their feelings about topics discussed; and, generally, focus as a team on the instructional needs of pupils.

Teachers on interdisciplinary as well as exploratory teams find these periods an excellent opportunity to discuss specific discipline problems. Teachers on a team may form a common set of rules which pupils know will be uniformly applied. Parent conferences can be held during the planning periods, and the guidance counselor, principal or assistant principal can attend team meetings to discuss various topics or problems. The team leader is responsible for the effective use of planning periods.

Activities:
1. As a district or school, a policy statement should be created to decide the number of planning periods per week per team. This might vary by grade level and/or by subjects included in a given team.
2. Develop a set of guidelines or a checklist so that teachers will have specific examples of what should occur during the team planning period. Create a process to monitor the extent to which appropriate activities occur.
3. Using videotapes and a mentoring system, prepare a staff development program to help teachers learn and refine the skills needed to function as a member of a teaching team.

Using the Schedule Effectively. Once the master schedule is constructed, the major parameters of the program are created and defined. Block-of-time scheduling facilitates large and small group instruction as well as the constant re-grouping of pupils within the sections of a team. Teams may decide to rotate the sections so that no section has the advantage or disadvantage of having a subject first or last period each day. Teams will typically use a modular base to sub-divide the total block-of-time into more workable spans of time. This modular approach is responsive to the attention span limitations of the students as well as the desire of team members to provide a total, comprehensive program.

Flexibility is a key word in the middle school. The scheduling mechanism must be flexible enough to accommodate varying needs, yet facilitate the total program. In the final analysis, the team is responsible for creating the daily or weekly schedules to meet their students' needs. The greater this flexibility is exploited by the teachers, the more likely the program will be responsive to the varied, ever-changing needs of the pupils.

Another opportunity for teachers to respond to student needs is through re-grouping pupils for instruction within the schedule. Pupils should and can be in various types of groups during the day. These groupings can be changed according to the evolving needs of the population.

Activities:
1. Design an orientation program to familiarize staff members with the blocks-of-time that exist within the master schedule and how to use them most effectively.
2. Develop a statement for the philosophy and rationale defining the word *flexibility* and giving examples of how teachers are empowered to practice flexibility on a day-to-day basis.
3. Create a mechanism to monitor the extent to which teachers practice flexibility in the school as well as the school district. The purpose of this process is to reinforce the importance of flexibility within the middle school and to share examples of how this can be accomplished.
4. Design a policy statement for grouping and re-grouping students. In addition, an assessment is needed to ascertain the extent to which re-grouping occurs.

Sharing the Leadership Responsibility. Although many middle schools have team leaders assigned for the entire school year, there are many benefits of rotating the overall leadership responsibility among the various team members. It is also possible to sub-divide the various tasks in nearly equal fashion among all members. On an interdisciplinary team, one teacher could coordinate the skills program while another could be responsible for home-base activities. A third teacher could handle requests for parent conferences, while a fourth teacher could plan interdisciplinary activities.

Teams function best when all teachers accept responsibility for the successful operation of the team. Although it may be more feasible administratively to name one teacher as leader, middle school educators need to explore models that call for greater participation by all team members in the leadership function.

Activities:
1. Will each school have team leaders? Why?
2. What are the various functions that need to be accomplished by team leaders?
3. How can these tasks be shared?

SUMMARY

The team process is an integral part of the effective middle school. Although there is no research to indicate which is the best approach, it is evident that common factors in the team process enhance learning for early adolescent students. Since working on teams may be a new experience for many middle school teachers, staff development programs should provide the necessary assistance to be successful in this endeavor.

Chapter XIII
An Effective Middle School . . .

Emphasizes The Guidance And Counseling Function Of Staff Members By Providing For A Homebase Program, Stressing The Importance Of Self-Concept, And Providing A Positive Climate

One of the most important functions of an effective middle school is to meet the guidance and counseling needs of early adolescence. This guidance function is similar but different from the guidance and counseling programs typically found in elementary and high schools. Because of the tumultousness of the age group, the guidance function at the middle level is especially significant.

THE GUIDANCE AND COUNSELING FUNCTION

Guidance infers directing or managing. More importantly, the term guidance must be viewed as a concept, construct, and service. Conceptually, guidance involves the use of a point of view to help a middle school student. As a construct, guidance involves providing experiences to assist the early adolescent in self-understanding. Finally, as a service, guidance is a set of organized procedures and processes to achieve a helping relationship for middle school students.

Shertzer and Stone (1966) describe guidance as the process of helping individuals understand themselves and their world. This is not a single event but a series of actions or steps toward a goal. Helping involves preventing and remediating problems that may arise in the school setting on a developmental basis. Designed for all students, there is a clear focus on self-understanding and the need to assess the environment of the student as a basis for decision-making.

Anna R. Meeks (1968), a pioneer in elementary school guidance in the schools of Baltimore County, Maryland, defined guidance as a systematic approach for a more effective education through the active involvement of the child in the educational process. Dr. Meeks saw the school providing experiences to support the child's progress toward becoming an adequate person. She felt the school should help the child profit from opportunities available to realize the maximum of his or her potential. Designed to work for all students, the guidance program is a complement to the instructional process.

Dr. Meeks offered four major premises of an elementary guidance program that have definite implications for the middle school experience.

1. Guidance is an integral part of the total education process.
2. Guidance is concerned with the developmental needs of children and therefore is for all children.

3. Guidance is focused on the child as a learner in the educational setting of the school.
4. Guidance is a developmental continuum.

Shertzer and Stone reviewed the literature of the guidance and counseling movement and offered eight basic constructs:

1. Guidance is assistance to the individual in the process of development.
2. Guidance is based on the recognition of the dignity and worth of the individual and on the right to choose.
3. Guidance is assistance given individuals in making wise choices, plans, interpretations, and adjustments.
4. Guidance is oriented toward cooperation, not compulsion.
5. Guidance is a continuous, sequential educational process.
6. Guidance rests upon a comprehensive study of the individual in society.
7. Guidance is a function in which many people are active.
8. Guidance exists to help the student realize and actualize the best self.

A clear distinction exists between guidance and counseling. Guidance is a broad term applied to a total school program featuring a broad array of services designed to assist pupils in making satisfactory adjustments. The guidance service includes the provision for student appraisal, an information service, a program of individual and group counseling, educational and career planning, follow-up, referral, communication and consultation with parents, inservice for teachers, and academic placement. Group guidance involves the dissemination of information via presentations, discussions, as well as question and answer sessions.

Counseling is one aspect of the guidance service that focuses on a communication process to help individuals overcome obstacles to their personal growth. Blackham (1977) defines counseling as a unique helping relationship in which the client has the opportunity to learn, feel, think, experience, and change in ways he or she thinks are desirable. Counseling sessions or interviews typically include establishing rapport; defining the problems from the child's perspective; setting realistic goals that are limited, specific, and attainable; generating alternatives to solve the problem; and evaluating the process as well as the outcomes.

Group counseling, on the other hand, involves the counseling approach applied to groups, preferably fifteen or less individuals. The group offers the necessary support through the involvement of peers. At the middle school level, this is an important response to the social-emotional needs of the early adolescent.

Both guidance and counseling are designed for all individuals, not just those who exhibit abnormal behavior. Via various approaches, counseling helps essentially normal individuals remove frustration and obstacles interfering with developmental growth. Many counseling models stress positive individual strengths in a variety of situations. Counseling is designed to help individuals attain a clear sense of identity.

WHO IS RESPONSIBLE FOR THE GUIDANCE AND COUNSELING FUNCTION?

Within the middle school setting, a number of individuals or groups have direct responsibilities for the guidance and counseling function. These individuals include:

1. *School Administrators*

Within the individual school, a positive attitude on the part of the principal toward the guidance and counseling function is imperative. In organizing the school and implementing the curriculum, the administrator is responsible for a comprehensive guidance and counseling program designed to meet the unique needs of early adolescent students. The priority that the administrator places on a viable guidance program sets the tone for the school. Administrators are responsible for the supervision of the day-to-day work of the guidance counselors assigned to that building to insure that counselors have sufficient time to plan and implement a program.

2. *School Counselors*

With their special training, counselors must assume leadership in organizing and implementing all aspects of the guidance and counseling program. On a daily basis, counselors must be available to both students and teachers to provide a variety of services. In addition to helping to achieve school goals, counselors must identify and achieve a set of goals unique to their specialized training. They much reach each individual youngster through a clearly designed management plan. This plan should include the involvement of the counselors in the home-base program and other phases of the curricular experience.

3. *Teachers*

Teachers must play a major role in the guidance and counseling program of a middle school. With a background in early adolescent development and in some subject, the teacher must be committed to meeting guidance needs of students through the medium of that particular curriculum subject.

Although not a trained counselor, there are many times that the teacher will be approached by a student for help. In many cases, the teacher can merely offer an ear and help the student reach a solution; in other cases, the teacher must know when to refer a student to the school counselor. As a member of a group planning and implementing a home-base advisory program, teachers help youngsters face a plethora of developmental issues.

4. *Parents*

Parents play a role in the guidance program for the early adolescent student. In most cases, parents are the most knowledgeable individuals about the child and should share information with school personnel so that appropriate goals are established and ultimately evaluated. On the other hand, the school has numerous opportunities to help parents better understand the onset of puberty and thus the physical, intellectual, socialemotional, and moral development of this age group. The school helps parents understand the effect of the peer group on a child. By participating in parent discussion groups, serving on guidance advisory committees, attending numerous functions at school, and communicating regularly with the teachers, parents can play a very important role in the guidance and counseling experience for the middle grades.

5. *Students*

Students are both contributors to and beneficiaries of the guidance and counseling program. Participating in the home-base program, group guidance sessions, group counseling, peer tutoring, peer counseling, and other formal situations, the students are important contributors to the guidance and counseling experience for themselves and others. The peer group should be utilized in positive and constructive ways. On the other hand, students receive the needed help to survive this developmental stage in the most positive way possible. By involving students in the evaluation of the program, they can help to shape its future.

6. *Curriculum Specialists*

Middle school curriculum must be oriented to the developmental needs of students in such a way as to enhance self-concept. Each curricular area must be so designed as to provide opportunities for growth and development, concomitant with the needs of the students. Alexander's curriculum model enhances the guidance and counseling function.

7. *Referral and Community Agencies*

Various community agencies must be available to help middle school students in times of need. Mental health services, drug and alcohol rehabilitation programs, and child abuse agencies must support the school by being available to receive referrals from families in need. As part of a home-base experience, students should have opportunities to explore the services available. Specialists from these agencies may assist school-based personnel who have more generalized training. Work experiences for early adolescents in such agencies may prove to be a valuable opportunity.

8. *Members of the Superintendent's Staff*

Members of the Superintendent's Staff, as part of administering the total school district, must insure adequate funding for the guidance and counseling program at the middle school level. Additionally, they must help to implement and evaluate services needed that are unique to the age group. In many ways, the goals are achieved via a district-wide commitment to guidance and counseling on a PreK-12 basis.

ROLE OF THE COUNSELOR/ROLE OF THE TEACHER

In achieving the guidance and counseling function of the middle school, all faculty and staff members must be actively involved in a coordinated, harmonious program of pupil services. The spotlight must be on early adolescent students and the many ways that their developmental tasks can be fulfilled. Despite the organization of the school into various departments of instruction, the major goal is to enhance the student.

All teachers must be clearly aware of their responsibilities in focusing in on the needs of the individual student. The curriculum for English, social studies, mathematics, or science should be used as a means to an end. The content objectives for foreign language, art, music, technology education, home economics, and physical education must be seen as ways to enhance the development of the early adolescent. As curriculum is developed and evaluated, units of study must be constantly viewed in relationship to the developmental tasks of the age group.

As teachers and counselors work together on a daily basis, the focus must always be on enhancing the self-concept of each youngster. Home-base activities, extra-curricular organizations, the intramural program, and the selection of students for special honors must be ways to reinforce this focus. As teachers plan lessons, it is mandatory that they recognize their responsibilities in extending positive self-image, whether that child be gifted and talented, in special education, working below grade level, or in the standard program. As teachers and counselors organize for instruction, it must be evident that they are working to enhance the self-concept of every child with whom they work.

The guidance and counseling function is clearly a major curricular thrust. As teachers and counselors work to correlate content, identify skills to be emphasized, and plan specific units within the home-base program, they must keep in mind the guidance and counseling function. They must remember to focus on the child as a learner in the educational setting, to provide assistance to each individual, and never lose sight of the importance of the dignity and worth of each individual. The ultimate goal of the guidance and counseling function is to help each student first realize and ultimately actualize his/her true potential.

In addition to the joint effort of teachers and counselors working together to make the guidance and counseling function a living philosophy within the building, there is the need to identify certain unique responsibilities of the counselor as well as of the teacher. With specialized training, the counselor . . .

1. helps all staff members focus on the physical, intellectual, social-emotional, and moral needs of the early adolescent learner. In addition to providing information to facilitate understanding the age group, the counselor helps all staff members identify the implications of these data for the day-to-day operation of the school.
2. provides individual and group counseling to students and their parents. In many cases, this is in response to teachers' referrals. Groups may be established for various purposes.
3. helps all staff members to recognize the uniqueness of individuals and the full potential of the middle school concept for meeting the varied needs.
4. provides group guidance sessions which supplement the home-base program.
5. serves as a consultant to teachers and teams. In the middle school setting, guidance counselors have the opportunity to work as integral parts of all teaching teams.
6. coordinates the registration of students for the next grade.
7. serves as a consultant to administrators, teachers, and parents.
8. plays a major role in the organization of the home-base program.
9. helps to coordinate the pupil appraisal program. Especially during the time of such major changes in students, counselors should be involved in gathering data and in helping to interpret those data.

10. orchestrates a career development program unique to the developmental stages of middle school students. One approach is via the home-base program; the other approach is within the context of the various instructional programs of the curriculum.
11. participates in parent conferences with teachers.
12. assists in grouping and re-grouping pupils for varying instructional purposes. In addition to the initial academic placement, counselors can play a key role as teachers re-group students for required and/or elective programs.
13. supports program evaluation as well as local research.
14. assumes prime responsibility for articulation with feeder schools.
15. participates in the Pupil Services Team Conference, a program designed to ameliorate complex cases requiring a multi-disciplinary approach to problem solving. The admission, review, and dismissal aspects of the special education program can also be accomplished through this structure.
16. refers to other agencies as needed.
17. utilizes staff development opportunities to help teachers learn appropriate guidance, counseling, and communication skills.
18. contributes to public relations through many contacts with parents, community leaders, and others.

By virtue of their specialized training and the opportunities to work in one-to-one and small group settings, counselors are key persons in establishing, implementing, and evaluating the extent to which the guidance and counseling function is an integral part of the middle school program. The counselors are not, however, the only ones with major responsibilities in this area. Teachers are the first line professionals to come in contact with students and to really make the guidance and counseling function an integral aspect of the middle school experience.

In addition to being responsible for teaching a particular course, teachers have a major obligation to implement the guidance and counseling function by:
- being committed to understanding and supportive of early adolescent students
- utilizing opportunities to present personal development topics in the curriculum that are appropriate to the developmental needs of students
- taking advantage of opportunities to establish rapport, communicate, and counsel students
- utilizing the skill development aspect of curriculum to address specific needs of youngsters
- making referrals to the counselor when appropriate
- implementing suggestions from the counselor to help a student in a given situation
- providing input to the teaching team on the developmental needs of students
- attending the Pupil Services Team to help those professionals better understand the unique needs of students
- planning and implementing an effective home-base program

- utilizing opportunities to have one-to-one and small group contacts with students
- offering tutorial assistance where appropriate

Although primarily a subject matter teacher and a member of an instructional team, the classroom teacher can contribute greatly to the guidance and counseling function in the middle school. In most cases, it is the classroom teacher who knows a youngster better than any other person in the building. Teachers can play a very important role in reinforcing the guidance and counseling function as they interact with students on a daily basis

Obviously, the guidance and counseling function is a major tenant of the middle school concept. When all professionals in a building work together toward this end, the success is evident to all.

ACTIVITIES

1. How will this school district or school define the guidance and counseling function? How will this be related to the unique needs of middle school students? How will this be incorporated into the philosophy, goals, and rationale statements? How will this element be evaluated?
2. How will the guidance and counseling function reach all students? Develop a management plan for grades 6 through 8 to include all professionals in the building. Include plans for the transition from elementary to middle school as well as from middle to high school. Within this management plan, differentiate between the guidance and counseling activities of all staff members.
3. For each of the four premises of Dr. Meeks and the eight constructs of Shertzer and Stone, list four specific ways in which the guidance and counseling program can respond to the unique needs of the middle school student.
4. For your school and/or school district, list the specific responsibilities for the guidance and counseling program assumed by school administrators, counselors, teachers, parents, students, curriculum specialists, referral and community agencies, and members of the superintendent's staff.
5. For your school and/or school district, define the specific role of the guidance counselor as well as the role of the classroom teacher in achieving the guidance and counseling function. How will these roles overlap in your setting? Develop a procedure to assess the items on each list.

HOMEBASE PROGRAM

Known also as the teacher/advisory, advisor/advisee, or homeroom/advisory program, the home-base program is a fundamental component of the guidance and counseling function in the middle school. An extension of the elementary classroom guidance program, this program affords opportunities for students to learn about themselves as they go through the trials and tribulations of puberty and the early adolescent period. A number of issues and strategies will be presented as a review of the literature and as a guide to the implementation and administration of a viable home-base experience that responds to the needs of early adolescents.

Organizational Considerations

When developing this program, a number of questions should be answered. Via the staff development program, all staff members should contribute to resolving these questions.

All Teachers. Should all teachers participate in the home-base program or should this be restricted to the teachers of interdisciplinary teams? A factor in answering this question is the opportunity to plan for this phase of the curriculum. Specifically, will there be an opportunity for staff development so that every professional in the building can receive the necessary training?

Secondly, do all teachers in the building have a commitment to support the home-base program? If this commitment is shared among all staff members, all may participate. If, on the other hand, a school is starting a pilot project and/or has a limited number of truly enthusiastic teachers, it may be best to organize the home-base program as a function of the interdisciplinary team.

A third factor is the commitment of the school district to this program. If there is a solid commitment for this aspect of the middle school concept, there may well be advantages in involving all teachers.

Interdisciplinary Team. The home-base program may be the heart of the personal development phase of curriculum and could easily be delivered by the interdisciplinary team as they implement this model on a daily basis. The student/advisor ratio will be higher than desirable. Another reason for using this approach is the block-of-time from which appropriate amounts of time for the advisory component can be allotted. Finally, teachers will be able to correlate the content of the advisory curriculum with their individual curriculum presentations.

Flexible Scheduling. In some school districts, a definite amount of time is established for the home-base program. This may be the equivalent of as few as one or as many as five periods or mini-periods per week. In these cases, a modular approach to the time factor may or may not be needed. In other cases, a definite amount of time may not be established; thus, it is necessary to subdivide the total block-of-time to identify opportunities to present this program.

Definite Periods Per Week. Perhaps the greatest opportunity for the success of the home-base program is when there is a definite time allocation. The commitment to the home-base program as a viable part of middle school curriculum is made known when a minimum of one to a maximum of five periods per week are designated for this purpose. Some school districts utilize an eight period day as a method of providing for this aspect of curriculum. Without a definite number of periods per week, the success of the advisory program is at the mercy of a group of teachers in an individual team or school. Such variance may work against the needs of early adolescent children. The length of the period for home-base may be less than a regular instructional period.

Definite Curriculum. In most cases, schools or districts provide a curriculum guide for the home-base program. The guide typically consists of a number of units which are then sub-divided into lessons by grade level. Teachers find such a curriculum guide or cookbook approach helpful in preparing for these lessons. Other districts leave the curriculum issue up to the individual school or team. Although this approach allows for creativity on the part of teachers, it also creates apprehension and a need for teachers to plan home-base lessons on a regular, systematic basis. Some teachers may not be as enthusiastic as others in accepting this added responsibility.

Class Size. An advisory group may be a regular sized class, although it is preferable for an advisory group to be much smaller. Consideration should be given, therefore, to including enough professional personnel as advisors to reduce class size to facilitate discussions, opportunities for individual consultations, and opportunities for peer counseling within the varied structure of the advisory group.

Ungraded. Another major consideration is whether or not the advisory group should include students of more than one grade level. Obviously, there is benefit to a student to have the same advisor for the three years of the middle school experience. It is also beneficial to include students of various grade levels in the advisory group. Seventh and eighth graders could serve as mentors to sixth graders. Positive role models for study habits and conflict resolution would be available within this heterogeneous arrangement. Greater opportunities for peer tutoring and counseling exist within this ungraded model.

Home-Base Advisory Committee. In an effort to coordinate this program, many schools establish a home-base advisory committee which typically consists of teachers, administrators, counselors, parents, and central office curriculum specialists. In some situations, students are invited to attend. This committee develops the curriculum, acts on concerns, and coordinates needed staff development.

Staff Responsibilities

In this example provided by the Middle Country School District, Long Island, New York, specific responsibilities of the school administration, counselors, and teacher-advisors are listed. These may serve as a model for other school districts seeking to identify specific responsibilities.

Administration
- To generate a total school philosophy that supports the home-base program
- To promote home-base programs within the school and community
- To provide appropriate inservice training
- To develop a management system
- To allocate time and space within the school for planning and implementing various dimensions of home-base

Counselors
- To coordinate the home-base program
- To help in the motivation and development of activities
- To coordinate inservice training for advisors
- To accept referrals from advisors
- To communicate with advisors about their advisees
- To serve as a resource person for teacher-advisors

Teacher-Advisors
- To provide a warm, caring environment to achieve the goals of the program.
- To implement specific home-base activities
- To be a good listener and respond to the needs of the students
- To refer students to their guidance counselor and keep the counselor informed of the students' progress
- To attend staff meetings concerning advisees
- To assist and encourage advisees' academic, personal, and social development
- To keep appropriate records

In general, a caring advisor demonstrates good communication skills, sees and accepts early adolescence as a significant stage of human development, recognizes the home-base program as an integral part of the middle school program, enjoys the company of early adolescent students, correlates the home-base program with his/content area, and utilizes appropriate teaching strategies for early adolescent students in all dimensions of the program.

Statement of Beliefs

As an integral part of implementing staff development for the home-base program, a school district and/or individual school should collectively compose a series of "We Believe" statements. An example is provided from the materials of Middle Country School District, New York.

WE BELIEVE . . .

. . . All students need close personal contact with an adult outside of the academic curriculum.

. . . Students need guidance to accept responsibility for the consequences of their own behavior and its effects on others.

. . . By sharing a relationship based on mutual respect, concerns, and goals with an adult advisor, students will be able to develop valuable skills in self-awareness, communication, self-direction, and positive self-esteem.

. . . The school environment should be structured so that students recognize it as one that is responsive to their needs.

. . . Advisory periods should be enjoyable and should provide increased social interactions while celebrating the joy of learning.

. . . A successful advisory program will be beneficial for all students, teachers, staff, and parents.

. . . Communication between and among students, teachers, staff, and parents is vital to a healthy school atmosphere.

. . . A student-centered educational program values both subject matter and human relationships.

. . . Students, with the help of their advisors, should learn how to monitor their academic progress.

. . . Students need to be aware of the effects of the great personal changes of adolescence.

. . . Students and staff should be encouraged to recognize and appreciate the unique contributions, rights, responsibilities, and esteem of self and others, regardless of individual differences.

. . . The improvement in the home-base program will come from on-going planning which is the result of periodic reexamination and revision of policies and priorities in all curricular and extra-curricular areas.

Who Will Write the Curriculum?

In many schools and school districts, those responsible for the home-base curriculum borrow or utilize units developed by other schools or school districts. Although this is a convenient way to start the program, there is a trend toward individual schools or school districts creating their own home-base curriculum. In these situations, a committee is formed consisting of teachers, counselors, school administrators, and central office curriculum specialists.

As these materials are developed, it is crucial for teacher-advisors to participate in inservice courses to become familiar with the materials, learn how to present them, and become actively involved in a process of assessing the effectiveness of specific lessons for specific students. In many cases, teachers are given an initial outline; and, during summer workshop experiences, actually participate in writing the curriculum.

The format for the curriculum should be such that teachers can refer to lessons in a cookbook fashion. Many teachers are willing to teach these lessons but do not feel they have the time to design the lessons. Thus, the "add water and stir approach" is acceptable to middle school teachers who are working hard to implement all phases of the middle school experience and for whom home-base is a new experience.

Frequently, teachers may choose to have discussions and utilize peer counseling models in lieu of this preplanned curriculum. Schools or school districts should develop policy for the percent of time that formal lessons should be taught and the amount of time that can be allowed for discussions.

Some Possible Home-Base Units

In designing a home-base curriculum, the following topics may be developed into units. Some of units can be repeated in all grade levels; some may only be appropriate one time.

1. Orientation
2. Resolving Conflict
3. Study Skills
4. Communication Skills—Written and Oral
5. Enhancing Self-Concept
6. Drug and Alcohol Resistance Education (D.A.R.E.)
7. Decision-making
8. Understanding Myself and Others
9. Getting Ready for High School
10. Growing Up in Various Cultures
11. I Am Lovable and Capable (IALAC)
12. Understanding Similarities and Differences

13. Helping the Handicapped
14. Interpersonal Relationships
15. Compassion
16. Courtesy
17. Honesty
18. Human Worth and Dignity
19. Integrity
20. Justice
21. Loyalty
22. Respect for the Rights of Others
23. Self-Management: Rights and Responsibilities
24. Self-Management: Planning
25. Team Building

ACTIVITIES

1. Using the eight factors listed under the heading of *Organizational Considerations,* develop a position paper on the implementation of the home-base advisory program for your school or district. The position taken should reflect as many of the eight factors as possible.
2. As a simulation, conduct an initial meeting of the Home-base Advisory Committee to identify responsibilities of administrators, teachers, and counselors. Describe specific responsibilities as well as personal characteristics helpful to the success of the program.
3. Compose a Statement of Beliefs for your school or school district.
4. Conduct a second simulated meeting of the Home-base Advisory Committee to decide who will write the curriculum. List all alternatives considered, the final decision, and why that decision was made. Then, create a plan to present that decision to the School Board.
5. Review the list of possible units. Are there some to be added? Are there some to be deleted? Decide which units will be taught for the first three months of the school year and develop a plan to compose the curriculum and train the faculty.

THE IMPORTANCE OF SELF-CONCEPT

A key factor in fulfilling the guidance and counseling function in an effective middle school is the focus on self-concept throughout all aspects of the middle school experience. Teachers must both respect the dignity of each individual and recognize that each middle school student is in the process of developing and/or re-examining a look at self.

Snygg and Combs (1949) state that all behavior, without exception, is completely determined by and pertinent to the phenomenal field of the behaving organism. In other words, how a person behaves is related to how that person perceives the situation and himself at the time. How a person feels and thinks determines the course of action, not the facts.

Self-concept is an extremely critical issue during the early adolescent period. As the physical and physiological changes occur, former beliefs as a child may be shattered. The early adolescent is aware of these changes and is not certain of adult roles that may be expected. The middle school years offer a time for the exploration of behaviors and lifestyles. Drug use, eating disorders, pregnancy, crime, and attempted suicide may be among the thoughts of the early adolescent. This is a time period with a great degree of uncertainty. In some cases, young people may not have a cognitive picture of the real self; and, in most cases, the peer group really affects self-concept. All of this is compounded by the search for independence, the move away from dependence on adults.

Middle school educators must carefully study the literature on self-concept and recognize the major impact that self-concept development has on patterns of early adolescent behavior. Beane and Lipka (1987) encourage middle school educators to create a self-enhancing school. They define a self-enhancing school as one which helps young people to clarify their self-concepts, develop positive self-esteem, formulate values, and understand their relationship to the social world around them.

Beane and Lipka recommend five general objectives to help middle school educators enhance self-esteem among middle school students.

1. Develop clear and accurate self-concept
   – recognizes personal strengths and limitations
   – applies self-evaluation skills adequately
   – is able to describe self without difficulty
2. Develop constructive values as sources of positive self-esteem
   – has clear values and beliefs
   – respects dignity of self
   – is concerned for welfare of others
   – listens to views of others and is open to new ideas
   – thinks carefully about value issues
3. Understand importance of self-perceptions in living and learning
   – knows that positive self-esteem is a key factor in self-respect
   – understands that positive self-esteem leads to satisfaction with life
   – is able to envision satisfactory life plans
   – strives for mental health
4. Develop skills for self-evaluation
   – knows techniques for self-assessment
   – adequately applies self-evaluation techniques
   – demonstrates continuous self-assessment
   – recognizes personal strength as well as limitations
5. Understand physical, social, and cognitive changes and how they affect self-perceptions
   – accurately describes stage developments in transescence
   – accepts reality and inevitability of transescent stage developments
   – accurately describes developments in childhood and adolescence
   – knows difference between controllable and uncontrollable events in transescence
   – recognizes that peers deal with similar events and concerns.

Middle level educators need to recognize the major educational implications of self-concept theory. Implications include:

- *teacher-student relationships*

Middle school students are greatly influenced by their interpersonal relationships with teachers. As significant persons in the lives of these students, teachers should be success-oriented, offer positive reinforcement, and realize that they are serving as role models at all times during the day. Teachers also are in a position to control peer interactions within the classroom. They can help students to evaluate events that occur and learn from various experiences in and out of the classroom.

- *each curriculum area provides opportunities for self-concept enhancement*

By mastering content and acquiring skills, self-concept is enhanced. Middle school students need to see themselves as successful, capable of learning, and capable of growing or maturing as individuals. In many cases, students become adept in these content areas and benefit when others see them in such a positive way. This success can be transferred to other settings and can be the basis of future selections in the middle school, high school, college, or even as career choices.

- *home-base advisory program*

One of the major purposes of this program is to address key issues of development and self-concept enhancement for the early adolescent. The program should include a balance between cognitive information and opportunities to integrate that information into that perception of self. The advisor must get to know each advisee and, wherever possible, correlate home-base content with content in that teacher's curriculum area.

- *grading*

In many cases, grades assigned by teachers have a detrimental effect upon students; yet, grading is a necessary part of the learning process. In developing a grading system, school districts or schools should consider the unique needs of the early adolescent. Successful models should include a method of communicating all that the child has accomplished during a given marking period. Interim reports can be issued to keep students and parents informed of progress. The home-base program should address the affective issues related to the grading model.

- *developing a healthy self-concept*

The responsibility for helping each middle school student develop a healthy self-concept must be a total school effort. The focus on self-concept must be evident in all aspects of school life. Everyone who works in the school must look at how each act affects the self-concept of the students involved and must build bridges between family and school as positive support systems. Teachers must get to know the total child and strive to understand behavior in the most comprehensive way. Making a mistake is acceptable; teachers must show students that risk-taking is a good idea. Teachers should be accepting and success oriented, not judgmental.

ACTIVITIES

1. Develop a comprehensive definition of self-concept to guide the middle school years program.
2. Evaluate the school as a self-enhancing school. Include curriculum, student-teacher relationships, the home-base program, and other factors.
3. Using the general objectives of Beane and Lipka, develop a plan to achieve the five areas.

4. Develop a position paper on one or more of the implications of self-concept theory. In that position paper, be sure to include how the objectives will be accomplished.

PROVIDING A POSITIVE CLIMATE

A positive climate reflects the guidance and counseling program and the commitment of the school to enhancing the self-concepts of early adolescents. Purkey and Novak (1984) describe an invitational model to guide the implementation of a positive climate. Invitational education is based on four principles: (1) people are able, valuable, and responsible and should be treated accordingly; (2) teaching should be a cooperative activity; (3) people possess relatively untapped potential in all areas of human development; and, (4) this potential can best be realized by places, policies and programs that are specifically designed to invite development and by people who are personally and professionally inviting to others.

The following activity is designed to help a school assess its climate as well as the extent to which the guidance and counseling function is being implemented.

ACTIVITY

1. In light of the literature and research, describe the ideal school climate for the needs of the early adolescent student.
2. Assess the climate of your school. How does the climate reflect the school's philosophical position on the guidance and counseling function, the home-base program, and the school's definition of self-concept development for the early adolescent?
3. If there is a gap between the ideal and the real, design a plan to improve the climate of the school. Be sure to identify the role and responsibility of all staff members and spread the goals over a reasonable time period.
4. Design a process to evaluate the climate of your school in three to five years.

Chapter XIV

An Effective Middle School...

Promotes Flexibility In Implementing The Daily, Weekly, And Monthly Schedule To Meet The Varying Needs Of Students

A key to success in implementing the middle school concept is the extent to which teachers use flexible scheduling. Initially, it is essential that the master schedule be constructed on a block-of-time basis; then, it is important that teachers use and feel comfortable with flexible/modular approaches.

Traditionally, the schedule in junior and senior high schools is characterized by sameness. As a result of Carnegie units and tradition, the order of classes is the same, and the time duration for each of the classes is the same. For grades 9 to 12, the principal must certify that a student attended each class for 50 minutes per day. Thus, because ninth grade credits count toward graduation from high school, the organization of the high school determined the junior high school schedule. Junior high teachers were unable to shorten or lengthen a class period, change the number of periods in a given day, change the order of the periods within the day, or do other innovative activities because each class had to be 50 minutes in length.

In the middle school, such rigidity is not necessary. Even if ninth graders are assigned to the middle level school, the concept of flexibility can be implemented in the other grades. Flexibility is a response to the rapid physical growth, short attention span, fatigue, and reality that students are at different stages of development. Without a concern for Carnegie units, middle school teachers can plan the instructional program according to the unique and varying needs of students.

WHAT IS FLEXIBLE SCHEDULING?

The term *flexible scheduling* suggests that the order of each day need not be the same and that students can be in various grouping arrangements during the course of the day, week, month, or year. Group size can vary, the order of the periods can vary, the length of each period can vary, and the student can be in one group for mathematics and another group for reading.

Flexible scheduling, however, is not a concept that can be mandated by the school administration. Rather, once the provisions for flexible scheduling are put into place, it is up to the teachers to take advantage of the opportunity to be flexible. Some lessons should be 30 or 35 minutes in length; other lessons, if planned properly, can be 60 to 65 minutes. A student should not always have mathematics seventh period of the day. Physical education classes should be scheduled in the morning on some days and in the afternoon on other days. This variety is important for both teachers and students. Although flexible scheduling requires many decisions by teachers about students' needs, content, and even teaching strategies, the approach should be viewed in light of the benefits for students.

Flexible scheduling is a concept, a point of view, and a basis for teachers to work together to achieve a common goal—the best possible learning experience for pupils. This chapter will introduce techniques for utilizing the block-of-time, creating rotating schedules, designing modular subdivisions of time, identifying local options, creating alternate day rotations, and grouping and regrouping students for various instructional purposes.

BLOCK-OF-TIME SCHEDULING

Block-of-time exists when two or more teachers of two or more subjects teach those classes during the same time period. In grade 6, two teachers may be assigned to two sections that have been scheduled on a parallel basis. One teacher would be responsible for English and social studies for both sections; the other teacher would teach mathematics and science to both sections. The teaching of reading would be a function of both teachers. In grade 7, an English, social studies, mathematics, and science teacher may have the same four classes for periods 1-4 each day. These teachers have, in essence, a total of 200 minutes of instruction for the 110 students on the team. Their schedule is such that they have common planning periods outside of the block, an essential feature.

There is a difference between interdisciplinary team organization and block-of-time. To be an interdisciplinary team, the teachers do not have to be scheduled at the same time; although it is most advisable, it is not mandatory. Block-of-time, on the other hand, requires that the teachers involved are teaching at the same time.

The following is an example of a block-of-time schedule for an interdisciplinary team.

BLOCK-OF-TIME SCHEDULE

PERIOD	MONDAY	TUESDAY	WEDNESDAY	THURSDAY	FRIDAY
1	8A			8A	
2	8A	8A	8A	8A	
3	8A	8A	8A		8A
	L	U	N	C	H
4		8A	8A	8A	8A
5			8A	8A	8A
6	8A	8A	8A		8A
7	8A	8A		8A	8A

Activity:
1. What opportunities are there for block-of-time scheduling?
2. Within the block-of-time concept, what subjects will be included within the interdisciplinary, disciplinary, and/or core/combination team arrangements in grades 6, 7, and 8?

3. What implications are there from these decisions for the construction of the master schedule?

ROTATING SCHEDULES

One of the benefits of the block-of-time approach is the opportunity to create rotating schedules. In the example provided in the previous section, there are five teaching sections for five subjects with five teachers; therefore, there can be at least five options, rotations, or sequences of classes through the various subjects of the interdisciplinary team. In this way, each teaching section can experience each of the options for an equal amount of time during the school year. If there are advantages or disadvantages for any of the options, all teaching sections can experience these equally. Rotations can be daily, weekly, monthly, or quarterly. The following grid provides an opportunity to create a rotating schedule.

PERIOD	TUESDAY Teaching Section/Subject
2	(1) ENGLISH (2) MATHEMATICS (3) SCIENCE (4) READING (5) SOCIAL STUDIES
3	(1) (2) (3) (4) (5)
4	(1) (2) (3) (4) (5)
6	(1) (2) (3) (4) (5)
7	(1) (2) (3) (4) (5)

Activity:
1. What is the commitment of the school to the concept of flexible scheduling?
2. To what extent does the administration of the school encourage the use of flexible scheduling?
3. Have the persons who built the master schedule provided block-of-time for each teaching team?
4. To what extent will teachers utilize block-of-time opportunities that exist?
5. What rotations are possible for each team?
6. How will teams evaluate their use of block-of-time?

MODULAR SUBDIVISIONS OF TIME

When the block-of-time concept has been utilized in the construction of a master schedule, the provision for modular subdivisions of time exists. A module refers to an amount of time other than the traditional 50 minute period. Modules can be 10, 15, 20, 25, 30, 35, or 40 minutes in duration. A modular approach can be used to divide blocks-of-time for various activities.

In grade 6, for example, the teachers may choose to utilize a 30 minute module for intensive spelling and handwriting instruction in addition to the regular program of studies.

12:00–12:30—LUNCH
12:30– 1:00—Spelling, Handwriting Activities
1:00– 1:40—Period 5
1:40– 2:20—Period 6
2:20– 3:00—Period 7

When modular subdivisions of time are used, the frequency and duration of class meetings are determined by teachers. These decisions should be based upon instructional tasks and needs of students. Teams of teachers are encouraged to think of all possible modular subdivisions of time as they plan a variety of activities to meet the unique learning needs of early adolescent students.

Activity:
1. Using the block-of-time schedule presented earlier in this chapter, create a schedule for Wednesday that allows a thirty minute home-base period and still permits all teachers to see all of their classes.

TIME	WEDNESDAY

2. Using the block-of-time schedule presented earlier, create a schedule for Monday that allows the team to introduce their skill-of-the-week and still teach each of their sections that day.

TIME	MONDAY

3. What opportunities for modular scheduling exist within our schedule?
4. What are some of the special needs of our students that can be met via modular scheduling?
5. How will we evaluate the effectiveness of our modular scheduling efforts?

IDENTIFYING LOCAL OPTIONS

Teams of teachers may identify optional programs in response to the needs of students. These local options are supplemental experiences to the required curriculum. Some examples of local options are:

(1) Home-base or teacher advisory (if not scheduled as part of the regular curriculum)
(2) Skills lab program
(3) SQUIRT—Sustained, Quiet, Uninterrupted, Independent Reading Time
(4) Extended homeroom to provide time for student government activities
(5) Spelling//handwriting

Activity:
(1) What local options do we wish to provide?
(2) How will we schedule these optional activities?

ALTERNATE DAY ROTATIONS

Another form of flexible scheduling is alternate day rotations, an approach that provides an opportunity for disciplinary and core/combination teams to be flexible. An example of an alternate day rotation is when an art and music teacher are scheduled on a parallel, block-of-time basis with the same 56 students for these two courses. On day one, half of the students are in each course; on day two, students attend the other course. Alternate day rotations permit teachers to combine classes when appropriate and regroup students according to student needs and the parameters of the program.

Typical alternate day rotations include:
- physical education/chorus
- foreign language appreciation/computers
- elective/physical education
- woodwind/art

Activity:
(1) What alternate day rotations exist in our schedule?
(2) How can we utilize these opportunities to improve our delivery of instruction?
(3) How will we inform students of these changes in the schedule?

GROUPING AND REGROUPING PUPILS

The final dimension of flexibility involves grouping and regrouping students for various instructional purposes. In some schools, a group of 25-30 students is known as a class and, for the most part, remains together for six or seven periods. In other schools, students are individually scheduled so that one could be in six or seven different groupings with as many as 150 or 200 different classmates each day. The effective middle school organizational plan should be somewhere between these extremes. Pupils can be grouped initially and then subsequently regrouped to respond to their ever-changing developmental needs.

Interdisciplinary teams can be grouped on a homogeneous and/or heterogeneous basis. If the grouping is homogeneous for all subjects, a pupil could be changed from one teaching section to another within that interdisciplinary team. If the grouping is heterogeneous for all subjects, pupils again could be changed from one teaching section to another, depending on the needs of the students. Another possibility is for the interdisciplinary team to be grouped homogeneously for some subjects and heterogeneously for others. Pupils in reading and mathematics classes could be grouped on a homogeneous basis according to achievement in those respective areas; social studies and science could be presented on a heterogeneous basis.

A final option for grouping or regrouping within the interdisciplinary team involves the parallel scheduling of two interdisciplinary teams. Teams 8A and 8B could be scheduled periods 3 through 7 each day. Cross team regrouping could be used to combine students homogeneously for reading and mathematics while retaining a heterogeneous arrangement for language arts, social studies, and science.

In disciplinary teams, pupils could be regrouped according to their progress in that specific subject. In physical education, for example, grouping could be dependent upon a student's ability and interests in that area. A student could be with one teacher for a gymnastics unit and in another setting for volleyball or soccer.

The three organizational patterns (interdisciplinary, disciplinary, and core/combination) are not mutually exclusive. The grouping decisions in each of these team settings are independent of the others; therefore, a student can be grouped and regrouped based on that individual's needs and performance factors in each teaming configuration.

Activity:
(1) How will pupils initially be grouped in each of these team situations?
(2) What are the school's guidelines on regrouping pupils for various instructional purposes?
(3) What procedures will our team follow when we regroup pupils? How will parents and students be informed of these decisions?
(4) How will we evaluate our efforts to group and regroup pupils?

SUMMARY

Flexible scheduling techniques permit teachers to develop a comprehensive program that responds to the needs of the pupils on that team. Block-of-time scheduling, rotating schedules, modular subdivisions of time, identifying local options, alternate day rotations, and grouping and regrouping pupils promote flexibility in implementing the daily, weekly, and monthly schedule to meet varying student needs.

Chapter XV
An Effective Middle School...

Actively Involves Parents In Various Aspects Of The School Experience

Parent involvement is a key element of an effective school. Numerous studies have revealed that children are at an advantage when parents have some measure of involvement in their schools. Unfortunately, not all parents know how to be involved, and not all schools invite parents to participate. Despite newsletters, special invitations, and telephone calls, some schools clearly give the message that parents are not welcome.

Although definitive research on the effect of parental involvement on academic success in the middle grades is lacking, there should be a more effective partnership built between school and home. As a first step in this direction, a number of myths should be destroyed. These myths include:
- parents of middle school students are not interested in the school program
- middle school students prevent parents from becoming involved in the program
- families of middle school students know how to be involved in various aspects of the program but choose not to be
- middle schools actively seek parental involvement
- inviting volunteers guarantees participation in various aspects of the middle school program

The reality is that there is a reduction in parent involvement as students move from elementary to middle school. The subject matter becomes more specialized, and parents may not feel adequate to help their children. Parent participation means communication with many teachers. Early adolescents, becoming more independent, may not seek the help of parents; they are more likely to turn to the peer group for advice.

RELATED RESEARCH

Dr. Joyce Epstein and associates (1987) have conducted studies which indicate that parents want to be involved in helping their children do well in school but need guidance about how to help. They need to feel more welcome. Hawley and Rosenholtz (1983) stated that parent involvement should improve student achievement. Research tends to support the premise that parental encouragement and participation at school will have a direct effect upon children's achievements, attitudes, and aspirations.

School officials must be clearly aware that not all schools actively seek parent involvement. Administrative leadership is a key factor in making parents feel welcome and in providing a variety of activities to help parents participate in the life of the school.

Epstein (1986) found that over 70% of the parents in a study were never involved in any activities assisting the teacher or staff at a school. Only 4% were involved at the school for 25 days or more per year. Although over 40% of the teachers in the study had some parental assistance in the classroom, this help was provided by only a few parents. Most parents feel that involvement in school is important, but only a few could assist on a regular basis. Further, the study showed that having some parents at the school positively influenced teachers' interactions with other parents.

Although most of the research related to parent involvement is aimed at elementary grades, John Myers (1985) concluded that the positive implications for parent involvement in middle grades were extensive. Myers points out that success for such programs depends upon two factors: (1) the variety of parent roles and (2) the need for long-term involvement.

WAYS TO INVOLVE PARENTS IN THE MIDDLE SCHOOL

To apply the research and counter the myths, middle level educators must be aware of ways to involve parents in the breadth and depth of the middle school experience. Throughout all these activities, principals and teachers must be intentionally inviting. Parents must clearly feel that they are welcome in the building and that all members of the school staff appreciate their contributions.

Among the many ways to involve parents are the following twenty approaches or programs:

1. *Volunteer programs.* Although many parents are working full and part-time jobs, there are opportunities to assist in some aspect of the school program. Training is needed for both new and returning volunteers. Parents feel comfortable when teachers offer bonafide opportunities for participation and appreciate the recognition given for their efforts.
2. *Provide a parent lounge in the school.* Parents appreciate having their own meeting place within the building. Bulletin boards can contain important announcements. This room can also be the meeting place for the PTA Executive Board as well as PTA committees. Appropriate reading materials about the school and the needs of early adolescents could be available in this room for parents to borrow.
3. *Informal gatherings of parents.* Especially for new, but also for returning parents, the school may host a breakfast, tea, or other social gathering to encourage participation of parents in a variety of activities during the course of the year. Parents should receive a calendar of events and learn how to become involved in specific programs. Parents should be made to feel welcome at these sessions.
4. *Dinner/sports nights for interdisciplinary teams.* Each interdisciplinary team could schedule an evening activity for its students and parents. A dinner, films, student presentations, materials review, or a sports event could be scheduled.
5. *Seminars on parenting early adolescent students.* Directed by guidance counselors, teachers, or school administrators, discussion sessions could address such topics as verbal communication, the challenge of authority, peer group influence, heightened emotional reactions, rapid physical changes, special needs students, and experimentation. Parents would have an opportunity to compare notes with

others parents. Parents of eighth graders could learn what to expect at the high school level. All parents could benefit from discussions of how the family and school can work together.

6. *Star of the hour.* Designed to combine student writing with parental involvement, parents can be invited to participate in a lesson that features their child's written composition. This approach gives parents an opportunity to view their child in a positive academic setting. After the lesson, the teacher and parents can discuss the student's academic strengths in that subject area.
7. *Publications.* A variety of publications will help parents to be fully informed of activities. School, team, PTA, and/or principal's newsletters complement the student newspaper as methods to keep parents informed. In addition, teachers may send home notices of special events. Calendars should be included in all of these publications.
8. *Individual conferences.* As part of monitoring progress of students, parents should be invited to meet with either the teaching team or the student's advisor at least once during the course of a school year. The focus should be on the development of the individual student and should feature participatory discussion so that both parents and teachers are contributing to and benefitting from this interaction.
9. *Telephone calls.* Both computerized and personalized telephone calls should be made to parents on a regular basis. Computer programs are available to call homes of students who are absent or late to school as well as to announce an important meeting or activity. Parents appreciate being called to receive a compliment as well as being notified when a project has not been submitted or a student's grades have dropped significantly in a particular class.
10. *Interim reports.* Report cards are typically issued every nine weeks. Parents also appreciate an interim or midquarter report indicating the student's status at that time. Some teachers only issue interim reports when a student is doing poorly; others issue an interim report to every student to notify parents of achievement midway through the marking period.
11. *Radio and television announcements.* Especially in small communities, radio and television stations are willing to publicize school events. Cable television is another source of publicity. Students can be involved in developing these announcements.
12. *Curriculum night.* Early in the school year, a "Curriculum Night" could be scheduled as a PTA program. In addition to meeting the teachers, parents can learn about the curriculum for that grade level, guidelines for home assignments, as well as the standards for promotion to the next grade.
13. *Special school/team events.* Despite work schedules, parents are willing to attend assemblies, performances, championship and all-star intramural games, and end-of-unit special activities. For example, as the culminating event of a science unit on oceanography, parents could attend an "Oceanfest" featuring an interdisciplinary approach to how people around the world rely on the sea for resources. Parents enjoy having lunch with their children and learning about the recently completed unit. They are also willing to chaperone field trips, dances,

parties, and activity days to gain a sense of the totality of the middle school program and to see how their child's development compares to that of others.

14. *Career day.* In conjunction with the homebase program and/or the guidance and counseling function of the middle school, parents can play an integral part in career day activities. They can describe the skills involved in their job and the training needed to reach that level. In this setting, parents become role models for other students.

15. *Assignments that actively involve parents.* Middle school teachers should give assignments that cause pupils to ask their parents questions or encourage students and parents to watch a television show together in order to answer specific questions. Such assignments will provide material to be used in the readiness portion of lessons, for concrete examples in the concept development process, and for application of content.

16. *Home study materials.* Parents can be involved in coordinating learning activities at home. These activities may be assigned by the teacher or initiated by the parents. Becker and Epstein (1982) reported 14 techniques, including asking parents to read to the child or listen to the child read, conduct discussions, play informal learning games, tutor in specific skills, and sign contracts to ensure that certain assignments are completed. In this program, more than 85% of the parents spent 15 minutes or more per day helping their child.

17. *Parent visitation day.* Although primarily for parents of incoming sixth graders, all parents should be invited to spend a day in the middle school. The purpose is to demonstrate to parents the excitement and vitality of the middle school experience. During these visits, parents should have an opportunity for active involvement in the learning process. They can lead discussions, check papers, or talk about skills needed for their jobs.

18. *Parent advocacy groups.* Parents should be involved in a variety of advisory committees, including the Library, Career Exploration Center, Special Education, and Home-Base Advisory Committees. In addition, parents can play a key role in committees designed to monitor the education budget, class size problems, textbook selection, or other issues.

19. *Guest speakers.* A parent committee can be formed to create a speakers' bureau. With sufficient notice, parents can assist in various aspects of the curriculum. In many cases, parents may continue to serve as resource persons beyond their child's enrollment at that school.

20. *Home visits.* In addition to parents visiting the school, school personnel may visit homes to discuss serious problems or to gain a perspective of the child's home environment. A pupil personnel worker, guidance counselor, teacher, or school administrator may make such a visit.

Activities:

1. Develop a process to measure the extent to which parents feel comfortable visiting the school. For example, a questionnaire can be

developed or parents can be interviewed before and/or after a visit to the school.
2. Develop a training program to sensitize teachers as to how they can make parents feel more comfortable in the building. Role plays and discussions may help teachers become more perceptive of parents' feelings. The training should also include analysis of how nonverbal gestures affect communication.
3. Using the twenty activities listed in this chapter, develop a checklist and begin to tally the frequency of those activities. Then, develop a plan to encourage the utilization of less frequently used activities.
4. Identify activities beyond the twenty listed and mail them to the author of this book for inclusion in the next edition.

Chapter XVI
An Effective Middle School...

Evaluates The Program On A Regular Basis And Makes Changes That Enhance Learning

Evaluation is an essential aspect of developing a new middle school program or expanding an already existing one. Major components involved are gathering data, assigning a value to determine the success of a middle school program, and then identifying ways to adjust or improve the program.

Thoughts about evaluating the program should begin at the time of initial design rather than waiting until the end of a one, two, or three year period. Also, evaluation can and should be conducted by teachers and other staff members who are involved in the middle school experience on a daily basis. Although outside consultants or evaluators can assist, teachers should be viewed as the basic resource in program assessment. The work of regional accrediting groups as well as consultants should complement the self-study conducted at the local school level.

Faculty participation is as vital in evaluating the program as it is in conceiving the program. With proper preparation and involvement, the evaluative process can be enhanced by a faculty that is motivated and committed to that process. This chapter will answer five key questions:

(1) Why is evaluation needed?
(2) What are the types of evaluation?
(3) Who should participate in the evaluative process?
(4) How can a structured questioning technique be utilized?
(5) What should be done with the results?

WHY IS EVALUATION NEEDED?

Middle schools are new in many parts of the United States and abroad. In many schools, new programmatic pieces are being developed at a rather rapid rate. It is important, therefore, that educators who design new programs also think about assessment.

Evaluation can be the means of testing the many concepts or hypotheses underlying the middle school concept. One purpose of evaluation is to determine how well the school is implementing the middle school concept or achieving the goals established for the first year of the program. Factors such as interdisciplinary teams, home-base activities, skill programs, and healthy self-concepts should be investigated in greater detail at the local level.

Other purposes of evaluation include the opportunity to provide feedback to parents and the community; to create a listing of the strengths and weaknesses of the middle school program after one, two, or three years of implementation; to provide feedback to teachers on their efforts; to compare the efforts of one school with the efforts of other schools and districts in various parts of the country; and to obtain a view from outside sources of the progress in implementing the middle school program.

Activity:
1. Why do we want to evaluate our program?
2. What aspects of our program can be evaluated?
3. What areas of the program warrant our immediate attention?

WHAT ARE THE TYPES OF EVALUATION?

Alexander (1969) describes two types of middle school evaluation—formative and summative. Formative evaluation takes place during the initial stages of implementing the middle school concept. The feedback is used to make modifications or to gain support for the efforts of teachers and staff on behalf of the students. Specific school goals should be assessed periodically. An instrument should be developed to determine if the school is, in fact, providing opportunities for students to benefit from the new organizational plan.

From the rationale developed by the faculty, teachers could examine the extent of content correlation within the interdisciplinary teams, use of flexible scheduling, or time allotted for the home-base program. Formative evaluation should be used to identify whether or not the school has been successful in developing the type of middle school experience intended. It can take place from the outset of the transition through maturation.

As an example, Dr. Gerald Foley commissioned an evaluation of the five goals that highlighted the transitional year in the Middle Country School District, Long Island, New York. The evaluation called for central office and school based personnel, parents, and students to help examine the extent to which the five objectives were achieved.

The objectives were:
(1) to create a school setting that concentrates on both academic achievement as well as affective education
(2) to provide a smooth transition for sixth grade students, their parents, and their teachers
(3) to point out advantages of the middle school concept to seventh and eighth grade teachers
(4) to blend the sixth, seventh, and eighth grade faculty groups into one cohesive unit
(5) to eliminate pull-out programs

For each objective, respondents were to identify indicators that the objective was or was not fully achieved. Using results of the written self-evaluation and the on-site interviews, evaluators were able to provide Dr. Foley with data to help in assessing the extent to which each of the objectives was met.

Summative evaluation takes place after the middle school program has been developed and is fully operational. Summative evaluation, for example, could help to find out what happens to pupils after they attend a middle school. Other potential topics to be included in summative evalua-

tion efforts are:
(1) How do pupils who complete a middle school experience in grades six, seven, and eight perform in grades nine and ten?
(2) Does attendance at a middle school lower the risk of students dropping out of high school?
(3) Do middle school teachers use a greater variety of teaching strategies than other teachers?
(4) How is the personal adjustment of early adolescents enhanced by the home-base program?

Activity:
1. List three formative evaluation projects for the current school year.
2. List three possible summative evaluation projects to be considered by the faculty.

WHO SHOULD EVALUATE?

Evaluation should not be seen as the sole domain of outsiders but rather a function of local school staff, central office leaders, representatives of the community who have special interests or expertise in the middle school program, and outside consultants. Fullan, Miles, and Taylor (1980) suggest that teachers can and should play a critical role in evaluation. Teachers are knowledgeable about the many factors affecting student behavior and can provide insight to the success of various programs. Fullan, Miles, and Taylor state that a real key to developing support for an evaluation program is to give staff members and active role in developing the plan for assessment, creating instruments for the process, analyzing results, and implementing the recommendations.

Principals should also have input into the evaluation process. In many cases, it was the building principal who best understood the reason for developing a particular program as well as the key factors responsible for the success of a program. Once the data are received, principals can be a catalyst in implementing the changes suggested.

Others in the central office may play a key role in the evaluation process. A director of educational research, research advisory committee, director of middle grades education, director of curriculum and instruction, and/or a curriculum advisory council can assist the district level as well as local school efforts in assessment.

Frequently, consultants can be valuable resources. In many cases, these individuals are familiar with major evaluative models, the efforts to evaluate middle schools in other districts, and ways to resolve problems that may arise during the process. In many situations, it is helpful to have a neutral party conduct the various aspects of the evaluative process; but, consultants should seek to maximize the contributions of local personnel.

Activity:
1. Who will be on the evaluation committee?
2. Who will chair the committee?
3. To whom will the committee answer at the local school and/or central office levels?
4. What checks and balances exist to insure the involvement of teach-

ers and other local school personnel in assessing the effectiveness of the middle school program?
5. What is the role of the regional accrediting agency?
6. How will consultants be utilized?

HOW CAN A STRUCTURED QUESTIONING TECHNIQUE BE UTILIZED?

Johnston and Markle (1979) question the applicability of conventional measurement techniques in evaluating middle school programs. Paper and pencil tests do not lend themselves to assessing important middle level concerns such as self-concept, self-evaluation skills, curiosity, or interpersonal skills. Therefore, they point out, it is necessary to create less traditional techniques that can be applied to middle school situations.

Data for the unconventional approach may result from a process of structured questioning or interviewing so that the evaluator can reach valid and reliable conclusions about the effectiveness of a program. This format is suggested by Johnston and Markle as a general scope and sequence for a question-directed program evaluation:

1. **What are we trying to evaluate?** Precisely, what portion or component of the total education "package" are we most interested in assessing? Program evaluation will be more effective if specific components of the program can be identified. To illustrate, it is more desirable to define the object of evaluation as the "intramural athletic program" than "extracurricular activities."
2. **What do we expect this program component to accomplish?** What are the specific objectives of the program and what do we expect students to do as a result of their participation in the program? For example, the intramural program might be expected to encourage students to develop an affinity toward participation in athletics as a recreational pursuit.
3. **What will we accept as indicators that the program is achieving its objectives?** Can we list the student behaviors that will allow us to conclude that the program element has had a desirable impact? Is our intramural program, for example, attracting a large number of students? Do students participate in intramural-related activities outside of school? Do they attempt to improve their performance through self-directed practice?
4. **What sources of data are available which will indicate the presence or absence of the indicators?** What kind of data on student performance do we have? What kind must be collected? Do we have access to student records? Can we conduct structured observations? Can we utilize student self-report data? In general, what kind of data can be assessed in a reasonable period of time with manageable effort?
5. **What specific information from each source will be most valuable to our program evaluation?** Within each data source, what information is most clearly related to the objectives of the program? How can we gather, assemble, and organize this information?
6. **What do the data that we have collected tell us about our indicators?** Do our data lead us to believe that the indicators are present or absent?

What indicators are present?
7. **Based on the presence or absence of our indicators, what can be concluded about the effectiveness of the program?** Are the indicators of a program's effectiveness present in sufficient numbers and strength for us to conclude that our program is working? Can we justify our conclusions on the basis of data rather than personal opinion or the strength of our desire for the program's success?

WHAT SHOULD BE DONE WITH THE RESULTS?

Middle school educators should receive the data in an open, constructive atmosphere. If the evaluation instruments are developed with input from school-based as well as central office personnel, these people should be interested in seeing the data and identifying opportunities to improve the program. The strengths of the program should be used as a basis for further implementation of the middle school concept, and teachers should be motivated for additional professional development.

Evaluation should not be seen as an opportunity to blame or place responsibility for a weakness in a program. Rather, educators should work together as a team for improvement. When the results are positive, recognition should be given to those responsible for the success. The local media should publicize these successes.

There seems to be a relationship between the involvement of staff in the design of the instrumentation and the way in which the staff will respond to the data and implement changes. Local schools should realize this cycle and work to encourage a healthy approach to evaluation.

SUMMARY

Evaluation is a major aspect of developing effective middle schools. Faculty participation in this aspect of program development is at least as vital as the other phases. The direct questioning technique suggested by Johnston and Markle is a model that warrants further study and use by faculty groups.

EPILOGUE

The challenge facing middle level educators is to identify the most creative, innovative, and challenging ways to meet the unique learning needs of the early adolescent. New and exciting ideas are being implemented in a variety of settings; these ideas need to be shared with others interested in translating theory into practice.

More precisely, the real challenge is to actively involve teachers in the various phases of program development and implementation. Instructional leaders at the district and school levels must utilize the components of the change process and staff development to motivate teachers in implementing the middle school concept. Teachers will then accept these opportunities to participate in decision-making and assume ownership for the success of the program.

A number of components must be examined carefully in the process of developing a viable middle school experience. The areas to be included are: responding to the unique needs of the early adolescent, designing documents to guide the program, implementing an appropriate curriculum model, developing a program of studies based on exploration, focusing on transition with elementary and high schools, utilizing learning strategies that actively involve students, involving staff in the creation of a block-of-time schedule, instilling a guidance and counseling function that reaches all aspects of the school's program, utilizing flexible scheduling, involving parents in aspects of the school experience, and evaluating the program.

Naturally, the sequence of topics may vary according to the needs of a specific situation. It is impossible to implement all the characteristics at one time. Realistically, districts or schools should prioritize their efforts to respond to the unique needs of a given situation.

The real key to the successful implementation of the middle school concept is the extent to which teachers understand, believe in, and implement each of the component characteristics. With proper motivation and guidance, teachers can achieve the real potential of the middle school concept. When this occurs, teachers feel good about themselves as well as their efforts; and, perhaps most importantly of all, the school program becomes responsive to the needs of the student population.

BIBLIOGRAPHY

Alberty, Harold B. and Elsie J. *Reorganizing the High School Curriculum.* New York: McMillan Co., 1962.

Alexander, William et al. *The Emergent Middle School.* New York: Holt, Rinehart and Winston, Inc., 1969.

Baltimore County (Maryland) Public Schools. *1984 and Beyond: A Reaffirmation of Values.* Towson, MD, 1983.

Beane, James A. and Richard P. Lipka. *When Kids Come First: Enhancing Self-Esteem.* Columbus: National Middle School Association, 1987.

Blackham, Garth J. *Counseling: Theory, Process, and Practice.* Belmont, CA: Wadsworth Publishing Company, Inc., 1977.

Brookover, Wilbur and L. W. Lezotte. "Changes in School Characteristics Coincident with Changes in Student Achievement." East Lansing, Michigan: *Institute for Research on Teaching, College of Education, Michigan State University,* 1979.

Drash, Allan. "Variations in Pubertal Development and the School System: A Problem and a Challenge." *Transescence: The Journal On Emerging Adolescent Education,* IV, 1976, 25.

Edmonds, Ronald R. "Programs of School Improvement: An Overview." *Educational Leadership,* 40:3 December 1982, pp. 4-11.

Eichhorn, Donald. "The Boyce Medical Study." *Educational Dimensions of the Emerging Adolescent Learner,* ed. Neil Atkins and Philip Pumerantz, Washington: ASCD and Educational Leadership Institute 1973, 24.

Eichhorn, Donald H. *The Middle School.* New York: The Center for Applied Research in Education, Inc., 1966.

Epstein, Herman T. and Conrad Toepfer, Jr. "A Neuroscience Basis for Reorganizing Middle School Education." *Educational Leadership,* 36:8 May 1978.

Epstein, Joyce L. "Parent Involvement: What Research Says to Administrators." *Education and Urban Society,* 19:2 February 1987, pp. 119-136.

Epstein, Joyce L. "What Principals Should Know About Parent Involvement." *Principal (NAESP Journal),* January 1986, pp. 6-9.

Epstein, J. L. and H. J. Becker. "Teacher Reported Practices of Parent Involvement: Problems and Possibilities" *Elementary School Journal,* 83: November 1982, pp. 103-113.

Feinman, S. and R. Floden. "A Consumer's Guide to Teacher Development" *Journal of Staff Development,* 1:2 1980, pp. 126-147.

Flavell, J. *The Developmental Psychology of Jean Piaget.* Princeton: Van Nostrand-Reinhold Company, 1963.

Fullan, Michael. "Change Processes and Strategies at the Local Level." *The Elementary School Journal,* 85:5 1985, pp. 391-421.

Fullan, M., M. Miles, and G. Taylor. "Organization Development in Schools: the State of the Art." *Review of Educational Research,* 50:1 Spring 1980, pp. 121-183.

Fusco, Esther and Associates. *Cognitive Matched Instruction in Action.* Columbus: National Middle School Association, 1987.

Hawley, W. and S. Rosenholtz. "Educational Strategies that Increase Student Academic Achievement." Prepared for the U. S. Department of Education Office of Planning, Budget, and Evaluation, Washington, D.C., 1983.

James, Michael. *Adviser-Advisee: Why, What and How.* Columbus: National Middle School Association, 1986.

Johnston, J. Howard and Glenn Markle. "Evaluating Programs for Young Adolescents: An Unconventional Approach." *Transescence: The Journal on Emerging Adolescent Education,* VII, 1979, pp. 13-16.

Kohlberg, Lawrence. *Collected Papers on Moral Development and Moral Education.* Cambridge: Harvard University Laboratory for Human Development, 1973.

LaBenne, Wallace D. and Bert I. Greene. *Educational Implications of Self-Concept Theory.* Pacific Palisades, CA: Goodyear Publishing Co., Inc., 1969.

Lounsbury, John H. (Editor). *This We Believe.* Columbus: National Middle School Association, 1982.

Lounsbury, John H. and Gordon F. Vars. *A Curriculum for the Middle School Years.* New York: Harper and Row, Publishers, 1978.

Manlove, Donald C. (Editor). *Middle School/Junior High Evaluative Criteria.* Arlington: National Study of School Evaluation, 1979.

McPartland, James C. and Others. "Special Report on Middle Schools: A Description of Organizational Structures in Middle Schools and Their Effects on Student-Teacher Relations and Instruction." Reprinted from *CREMS Report,* June 1987, Center for Research on Elementary and Middle Schools, The Johns Hopkins University, Baltimore, MD, pp. 9-16.

Meeks, Anna R. *Guidance in Elementary Education.* New York: Ronald Press Company, 1968.

Merenbloom, Elliot Y. *The Team Process in the Middle School: A Handbook for Teachers.* Columbus: National Middle School Association, 1986.

Middle Country (New York) School District. *Programmed Advisory for Teachers and Students.* Centereach, NY, 1987.

Myers, John W. *Involving Parents in Middle Level Education.* Columbus: National Middle School Association, 1985.

Phi Delta Kappa. "Why Do Some Urban Schools Succeed? The Phi Delta Kappa Study of Exceptional Urban Elementary Schools." Bloomington, IN: Phi Delta Kappa, 1980.

Piaget, Jean. "Intellectual Evaluation from Adolescent to Adulthood." *Human Development,* 1: 1972, pp. 1-12.

Purkey, William Watson and John M. Novak. *Inviting School Success: A Self-Concept Approach to Teaching and Learning.* Belmont, CA: Wadsworth Publishing Company, 1984.

Rutter, M. and Others. *Fifteen Thousand Hours: Secondary Schools and Their Effects on Children.* Cambridge: Harvard University Press, 1979.

Shockley, Robert and J. Howard Johnston. "Time on Task: Implications for Middle Level Instruction." *Schools in the Middle.* National Association of Secondary School Principals. December, 1983.

Shertzer, Bruce and Shelley C. Stone. *Fundamentals of Guidance.* Boston: Houghton Mifflin Company, 1966.

Snygg, D. and A. W. Combs. *Individual Behavior.* New York: Harper and Row, 1949.

Steer, Donald (Editor). *The Emerging Adolescent: Characteristics and Educational Implications.* Columbus: National Middle School Association, 1980.

Sund, Robert B. *Piaget for Educators.* Columbus: Charles E. Merril Publishing Company, 1976.

Tanner, J. M. *Growth at Adolescence.* Oxford: Blackwell Scientific Publications, 1962.

Thompson, Charles L. and Linda B. Rudolph. *Counseling Children.* Pacific Grove, CA: Brooks/Cole Publishing Company, 1988.

Thornburg, Hershel. *The Bubblegum Years: Sticking with Kids from 9-13.* Tucson: Help Books, 1979.

Toepfer, Conrad F., Jr., "Areas for Further Investigation Suggested by Brain Growth Periodization Findings." *Transesence: The Journal on Emerging Adolescent Education,* VII: 1979, pp. 17-20.

PUBLICATIONS
NATIONAL MIDDLE SCHOOL ASSOCIATION

Developing Effective Middle Level Schools Through Faculty Participation. Second and Enlarged Edition
Elliot Y. Merenbloom (108 pages) $8.50

Preparing to Teach In Middle Level Schools
William M. Alexander and C. Kenneth McEwin (76 pages) $7.00

Guidance In The Middle Level Schools: Everyone's Responsibility
Claire Cole (34 pages) $5.00

Young Adolescent Development And School Practices: Promoting Harmony
John VanHoose and David Strahan (68 pages) $7.00

When The Kids Come First: Enhancing Self Esteem
James A. Beane and Richard P. Lipka (96 pages) $8.00

Interdisciplinary Teaching: Why And How
Gordon F. Vars (56 pages) $6.00

Cognitive Matched Instruction In Action
Esther Fusco and Associates (36 pages) $5.00

The Middle School
Donald H. Eichhorn (128 pages) $6.00

Long-Term Teacher-Student Relationships: A Middle School Case Study
Paul George with Melody Spreul and Jane Moorefield (30 pages) $4.00

Positive Discipline: A Pocketful of Ideas
William Purkey and David Strahan (56 pages) $6.00

Teachers as Inquirers: Strategies For Learning With And About Early Adolescents
Chris Stevenson (52 pages) $6.00

Adviser-Advisee Programs: Why, What, And How
Michael James (75 pages) $7.00

What Research Says To The Middle Level Practitioner
J. Howard Johnston and Glenn C. Markle (112 pages) $8.00

Evidence for The Middle School
Paul George and Lynn Oldaker (52 pages) $6.00

Involving Parents in Middle Level Education
John W. Myers (52 pages) $6.00

Perspectives: Middle School Education, 1964-1984
John H. Lounsbury, editor (190 pages) $10.00

Middle School Education: As I See It
John H. Lounsbury (64 pages) $5.50

The Theory Z School: Beyond Effectiveness
Paul S. George (106 pages) $6.00

The Team Process In The Middle School: A Handbook For Teachers, Second and Enlarged Edition
Elliot Y. Merenbloom (120 pages) $8.00

Middle Level Social Studies: From Theory To Practice
Michael Allen and C. Kenneth McEwin (56 pages) $5.00

This We Believe
NMSA Committee (24 pages) $3.50

Teacher To Teacher
Nancy Doda (64 pages) $6.00

The Middle School In Profile: A Day In The Seventh Grade
John Lounsbury, Jean Marani, and Mary Compton (88 pages) $7.00

Early Adolescence: A Time Of Change - Implications For Parents
Videocassette $75.00

Early Adolescence: A Time Of Change - Implications For Schools
Videocassette and Utilization Guide $80.00

NMSA, 4807 Evanswood Drive, Columbus, Ohio 43229
(614) 848-8211   FAX (614) 848-4301